The Law of
Balance

Thrive by Balancing Your Inner
Masculine and Feminine

LORAINE MAGDA

BALBOA.
PRESS
A DIVISION OF HAY HOUSE

Copyright © 2016 Loraine Magda.

All rights reserved. No part of this book may be used or reproduced by any means, graphic, electronic, or mechanical, including photocopying, recording, taping or by any information storage retrieval system without the written permission of the author except in the case of brief quotations embodied in critical articles and reviews.

This book is a work of non-fiction. Unless otherwise noted, the author and the publisher make no explicit guarantees as to the accuracy of the information contained in this book and in some cases, names of people and places have been altered to protect their privacy.

Balboa Press books may be ordered through booksellers or by contacting:

Balboa Press
A Division of Hay House
1663 Liberty Drive
Bloomington, IN 47403
www.balboapress.com
1 (877) 407-4847

Because of the dynamic nature of the Internet, any web addresses or links contained in this book may have changed since publication and may no longer be valid. The views expressed in this work are solely those of the author and do not necessarily reflect the views of the publisher, and the publisher hereby disclaims any responsibility for them.

The author of this book does not dispense medical advice or prescribe the use of any technique as a form of treatment for physical, emotional, or medical problems without the advice of a physician, either directly or indirectly. The intent of the author is only to offer information of a general nature to help you in your quest for emotional and spiritual well-being. In the event you use any of the information in this book for yourself, which is your constitutional right, the author and the publisher assume no responsibility for your actions.

Any people depicted in stock imagery provided by Thinkstock are models, and such images are being used for illustrative purposes only.
Certain stock imagery © Thinkstock.

Print information available on the last page.

ISBN: 978-1-5043-6209-2 (sc)
ISBN: 978-1-5043-6211-5 (hc)
ISBN: 978-1-5043-6210-8 (e)

Library of Congress Control Number: 2016911346

Balboa Press rev. date: 08/22/2016

For Simon...thank you
for believing in me and
helping to make this dream come true.

CONTENTS

Preface ix

Chapter 1: The Treehouse 1
Chapter 2: What is Masculine and Feminine Energy? 12
Chapter 3: My Balancing Act... 25
Chapter 4: Ten Benefits of Balance 40
Chapter 5: Is Inner Balance a New Idea? 60
Chapter 6: Can We Really Balance?....................................... 69
Chapter 7: Aren't We as a Society Balanced Enough?........ 83
Chapter 8: How Does the Gender Binary Affect Us? 107
Chapter 9: Case Study – Paulo 120
Chapter 10: How Balanced Are We as Individuals?........... 135
Chapter 11: What Does Balance Really Mean?................... 146
Chapter 12: The Journey-to-Balance Model........................ 157
Chapter 13: How Balanced Are You?.................................... 165
Chapter 14: Seven Steps to Balance...................................... 177
Chapter 15: A New Paradigm 184

Appendix A: Discussing the First Two Areas of the Model 193
Appendix B: Society's Journey to Balance............................. 201
Appendix C: More Examples of the Zig-Zag Tenet 205
Bibliography 215

PREFACE

"Gender fluidity" has become a modern buzzword. Although the term is not used extensively in this book its meaning is consistent with the message of the book: each of us has a masculine and feminine side that we are able to draw upon and utilize at will. When we do, it helps us to stand in our power – a creative, loving power – liberating us to develop our own unique potential and bring our gifts to the world. This is good for us, for everyone and the planet.

Inner balance is available to us but to benefit from it we must *choose* it. We need to befriend it and find comfort with the idea that we have a masculine and feminine side. Then we can take steps to integrate both sides, develop a relationship with each and bring them into a state of balance and harmony. This book will show you how with the aid of my unique Journey-to-Balance Model and Seven-Steps-to-Balance process.

Learning to cultivate inner balance – and harness it in your very being – enables you to be in the flow of your life and *thrive*. This is what I call the *Law of Balance*. I believe it is a law of nature just like gravity. This is what it states: a dynamic state of balance and harmony between your inner masculine and feminine is the key to thriving in every area of your life.

The reasons for the connection between inner balance and thriving are several and are addressed in this book. However, simply put, it works because you are in harmony with yourself, with nature and the universe. You are no longer working against yourself with an internal tug of war between your head and heart. You are fully aligned with yourself and this is how you come into your true power.

Much like the *Law of Attraction* which was unveiled and popularized in *The Secret* by Rhonda Byrne (1) and in *Ask and It Is Given* by Esther and Jerry Hicks (2), I believe it is time for the *Law of Balance* to be more widely recognized.

These two laws work closely together. Cultivating inner balance draws people, circumstances and events into your life that reflect your point of attraction. This is an expression of the *Law of Attraction*. Inner harmony reflects outwardly as being in the flow of your life and thriving. Your relationships and almost every aspect of your life are positively affected.

What about contrast and difference? Where does that fit in?

The *Law of Balance* acknowledges that you can explore contrast by immersing yourself in either masculine or feminine energy for a time – but if you want to thrive, you must return to your center. That is your "home base". This applies whether you are male or female and whether you are starting a business, writing a book, raising a family or moving to a new city.

While the concept of inner balance may be simple, carrying it out is not always easy.

One of the greatest obstacles to inner balance is social conditioning. The "gender binary" is the idea that depending on your biological sex you should either embody and express your masculine or feminine side, but not both. This is the status quo and it calls on us to be gender conforming. This message is reinforced by culture, religion and the media. It plays out in homes, families, relationships, schools, religious institutions, business, government, politics and in just about every echelon of society.

So not surprisingly, the idea that we each have a masculine and feminine side may affect people differently – some welcome it, others are open but uncertain about how to become balanced and others baulk at the idea. This book is not intended for the latter group. It calls upon us to step into new territory by opening up to more of who we are. As we all know, change can be scary. Yet, in these times there is arguably a great need to restore balance in the world. This has to start with us. We might as well learn how to do it – embrace the balance we wish to see in the world.

This book explores what it means to be balanced and how it will help you, your loved ones and the world. It also explores what inner balance is *not*. It paints a larger context within which inner balance makes sense but in the main it is intended to be a practical guide with examples to consider and manageable steps to try out.

What brings you to this book? Perhaps you are curious about what it means to balance the inner masculine and feminine. Or perhaps you are keen to discover healthier expressions of what it means to be a man or a woman in the 21st century.

Alternatively, if you have grappled with any of the following, then this book is also for you:

- Feeling habitually overworked, tired and unbalanced
- Relationship issues
- Living in your head
- Wanting to control life
- Trying to be everything to everyone
- Being assertive about your needs
- Not being entirely authentic
- Making a positive difference doing what you love

On the surface these issues may seem utterly different. Yet every one of them can be traced to an *internal imbalance*; either too much masculine energy unbalanced by the feminine, or the other way round.

This book explores this cause-effect connection and provides a unique approach to resolving these issues - not at the level of symptoms but at their source. This is a powerful way to create positive, life-changing results. Even a slight change at the source has a positive ripple effect.

Join me on this journey and discover the enormous benefits awaiting you.

CHAPTER 1

The Treehouse

As a child I would have preferred being a boy.

So much easier and more comfortable, I thought. The whole world geared up for you.

This is how I felt… until I discovered two things.

One - what feminine energy really is. Two – being in a particular body is not the problem. I could thrive in my own right and have the best of both worlds - if I chose. Anyone can. There is just one requirement: balancing the inner masculine and feminine.

But what does it mean to balance the inner masculine and feminine, and what are the benefits? My more than 40-year-long fascination with this topic has unfolded into this book. As it is becoming an increasingly hot topic in today's world, I felt called to share my discoveries.

I am happy to be a woman, one who is in touch with both sides of herself. This means enormous freedom. Being in touch with my masculine and feminine energies, I can simply dial them up or down in any situation, as needed. What freedom!

In recent history the idea of inner balance has been bandied about for the past few decades in progressive cultures. But as I discovered, knowing about it and living it are not the same thing.

Paulo, whose story appears later in the book, says:

> *I think there's a huge need... I think a lot of us are engaging with the idea of balancing our masculine and feminine energies. I don't know if we've yet got to a point where we have easy-to-use, everyday models that people can take on, to know how to become more balanced. It's all out there academically and in theory, but how does one bring it into practical application?*

That is what this book seeks to uncover.

As the topic of gender takes us to some of our most cherished and deeply-held ideas and assumptions, my suggestion is to take what works, and leave the rest. My desire is to share these discoveries so that you can benefit in your own ways.

This is my gift of love to the world. Its purpose is to assist those interested in balancing their masculine and feminine energies, and opening up to delightful new levels of abundance.

What is meant by masculine and feminine energies? Chapter 2 provides an in-depth explanation including the choice of the terminology, but here is a basic outline.

Masculine energies are outward-focused, active and differentiating tendencies such as being action-oriented, achievement-oriented, analytical, logical, focused, individualistic and assertive. These energies support us to put our stamp on the world.

Feminine energies are inward-focused, receptive and integrating tendencies such as the enjoyment of "just being", being relationship-oriented, intuitive, kind, empathic, seeing the big picture and going with the flow. These energies support us to create a rich and peaceful inner life and loving relationships.

These represent psycho-spiritual potentialities available to everyone - regardless of gender.

Can we be balanced?

For some, the idea of inner balance may be a confusing concept, and yet it has been encouraged by great minds since antiquity. How can I be in a male *or* female body and yet integrate my masculine *and* feminine energies?

This book will show it is possible.

Biology plays a role and creates differences between the sexes. But to what extent? Mark, an award-winning author and coach, believes we get to a point in our personal development where it is possible to "wear the cloak of your gender lightly."

The body is something to be enjoyed and experienced. But does it define you? My experience has shown that even while in a body we can be whole human beings. We are free to be much more, if we choose, than our biology suggests. While biology is a factor, our *thinking* plays a much larger role in who we become.

How did I arrive at this perspective, you might wonder?

For me it started with a treehouse.

Treehouse story

As a friendly and lively, but somewhat shy five-year old, I have just joined Kindergarten. Being the first day or two, I am still finding my way around. Having spent the morning baking "cookies" from play dough, I am now keen to play outside among the trees and sunshine. Eager to explore the playground during break-time I spot a treehouse with a ladder leading up and a pole for sliding down.

How cool! I think to myself.

I make a beeline for the treehouse. Having climbed the ladder onto the wooden landing, I slide down the adjoining pole much the way fire-fighters do.

Wheee! What a feeling!

After completing two such whirling descents a boy stomps up to me, hands firmly planted on his hips, and declares: "Girls don't do that!"

And with that, he stomps off again.

Unpacking the event

This interlude stopped me in my tracks. I had heard this kind of message before, about what girls (or boys) are and are not supposed to be or do. We know this as social conditioning. This one got my attention. Something was niggling me about this situation, something I couldn't quite put my finger on.

I felt highly conflicted: I wanted to fit in and be liked – just like everyone else. I also wanted to be free to choose my own pursuits.

As I glanced around the playground, indeed only one other girl was trying out the pole slide – and rather tentatively at that. Clearly I was the "different one."

Faced with the dilemma of what to make of all this, suddenly these words popped into my mind:

"God made me this way."

The words hit home with a powerful resonance.

Of course! God *must* have made me this way... created and endorsed my body for all its strength and athleticism or else I could not have had this particular one. Then the niggly bit came to light. Physically, emotionally and in every other way I was more than capable of doing *the very thing* that society (via this little boy) was trying to deny me because of its own idea of what my biological sex means.

Girls were supposed to be quiet, homely and to watch the boys climb up and down treehouses. Apparently they weren't supposed to do this themselves.

Yet, why would I deny my own abilities when they led to such enjoyment?

Then I realized it came down to a choice: I could be true to myself and risk the wrath of society *or* I could avoid rocking the boat but buy in to limiting ideas of who I am.

I decided to be true to myself as much as I possibly could. I would not always succeed - the lure of belonging, of wanting to fit in can be powerful - but it would be my mantra from that moment on.

Three insights

In retrospect, the treehouse episode resulted in three insights:

- I have inner masculine and feminine qualities. As Taoism indicates we all have yin (feminine) and yang (masculine) qualities.
- Society conditions and encourages us to be one or the other based on our biological sex.
- Being balanced is more fun, more effective and more beneficial.

To be in touch with my masculine side – my adventurous, assertive and sporty side brought different kinds of satisfaction and fulfilment than my feminine side did. Both were wonderful.

My feminine side - the part of me that enjoyed art, reading, music, visiting with friends or playing with my dog brought its own benefits.

I wanted to have it all, or at least have *access to it all* so I could enjoy a full, rich experience of life.

Being balanced when you're five years old is one thing; maintaining it through adolescence and into adulthood is another story. My journey to balance, with its twists and turns, rebelliousness and insights, is described in chapter 3.

Entering a new era

It is no coincidence that the topic of balancing the inner masculine and feminine is increasingly important in today's world. Beneath the noise and activity of modern-day living, something extraordinary is happening: a new era is being born.

Penelope, a 31-year-old business entrepreneur, whose story appears later, says:

> *I feel there is a consciousness shift. People are changing; their mentality, their energy. When I go back to London, I see it. A lot of my friends have shifted. A large portion of it has to do with the way we understand and manage ourselves. I mean just look at business. Everyone's wanting to go green.*

Nan Akasha, a business entrepreneur, coach and spiritual teacher, says (3):

> *I think for a lot of people right now the economy is shifting. The way that we used to do things – relate, make money, what fulfils us – everything has shifted and everyone is seeking something new.*

A revolution is taking place in the hearts and minds of millions.

The exciting part is that unlike the past two eras which were polarized – first toward the feminine (matriarchy) and then the masculine (patriarchy) - the new era is different. It represents a balance of masculine and feminine energies. This is the next step in the rise of our collective consciousness.

In his book *Power, Freedom and Grace*, renowned spiritual teacher and alternative medicine advocate, Deepak Chopra (4) says:

> *In cosmic consciousness… we begin to see that everything is a balance between feminine and masculine energies and anytime there is more of one than the other, we are out of balance. Right now, we need to reawaken the feminine because the dominance of the masculine has led to belligerence, arrogance, and aggression, the very problems we see in the world right now.*

Our shift into the new era is a move away from the imbalance of the previous era. I believe the new era begins to arise naturally once we have exhausted the learning that comes from imbalance and its excesses. Being on the cusp of a new era means we have reached a tipping point.

In her book *Healing the Soul of America* Marianne Williamson (5) describes an aspect of the new era:

> *In the century now dawning, spirituality, visionary consciousness, and the ability to build and mend human relationships will be more important for the fate and safety of this nation than our capacity to forcefully subdue an enemy.*

These spiritual leaders are saying the same thing: the new era requires moving away from the decidedly masculine worldview characteristic of the patriarchal era and restoring and raising the feminine in order to achieve a balance.

However, the emphasis on the feminine and letting go of the excesses of the masculine does not translate into: "feminine is good", "masculine is bad."

Both have the same potential for good or the lack thereof. The shift entails restoring the feminine to her rightful place as an equal, co-creative partner alongside the masculine. It is not about creating a new kind of imbalance.

Why is balance so essential to the new era? The synergies between masculine and feminine energies working in harmony will take us to new levels of life. By offering each other a healthy system of checks and balances, whatever is created from a place of balance can only be beneficial and provide for the greater good. This is the *Law of Balance*.

The benefit comes from taking the best of both and avoiding excesses of either.

We are already moving in this direction.

We now have better sharing of household and parental duties between working parents (though still not always equal); greater awareness around health and wellness; natural and alternative medicines; organic foods; cruelty-free products; animal welfare; conscious parenting; conscious business; sustainable living and green technology.

A call to balance

How does the new era affect each of us personally?

All of us are called to cultivate the *inner balance of masculine and feminine* that will give rise to, and reflect, the new era.

To usher in the era of balance, we first need to create it in ourselves.

While the idea of balancing the masculine and feminine energies may be daunting to some, this is an exciting time to be in because it represents a step closer to our true, spiritual nature.

According to Taoist philosophy, yin and yang are fundamental energies underpinning the entire universe and its workings. These complementary opposites, operating seamlessly in a dynamic and harmonious state of balance, reflect the nature of the Tao, or Source. They also reflect our own true nature.

To operate in harmony with the Tao, we are called to bring these two complementary opposites into a dynamic state of balance within ourselves.

Many Eastern and Western religions state that we are created in the image of God/Source/Spirit. Eastern spiritual traditions define our ultimate purpose as Self-realization, embodying our true nature as "Spirit in the flesh" and expressing our greatest potential – as God consciousness or unity consciousness - while in the body. What is important to realize is that this entails cultivating the *same* inner balance and harmony between masculine and feminine that occurs in Source. Since this potential exists at the deepest levels of our being, our job is to real-ize this, to make it real.

I believe integrating the inner masculine and feminine in a dynamic and harmonious state of balance is a *significant* milestone on the journey to Self-realization, yet is seldom spoken of in this context. This book aims to reveal the importance of inner balance on this particular journey that is the destiny of every soul in creation.

The end of false dichotomies

Could this be the end of the battle of the sexes?

How can it not be? Inner balance is the foundation for peace, harmony and collaboration between the sexes. It is accepting and embracing the masculine and feminine within us, around us and throughout the universe.

This acceptance also extends to those with different sexual orientations and gender identities. Making peace with the masculine and feminine within means being able to relate more easily to others regardless of outer shades of difference.

The new era is also the end of other false dichotomies such as science vs. spirituality; technology vs. the environment; western medicine vs. alternative medicine and profits vs. creating a better world. In each pair both sides are honored and the boundaries between the two are softened and blurred.

Cultivating inner balance across society would rapidly improve the world. War, gender inequalities, corporate greed, the growing gap between rich and poor, factory farming, animal cruelty and environmental destruction would dissolve.

The reason is simple. When people pose the question: "What would Jesus/Buddha/Mohammed/Lao Tzu/Quan Yin/Krishna/Mother Teresa do in this situation?" I offer this perspective: they would do what a wholly balanced being would do.

This is because masculine and feminine energy in their mature, balanced forms are *nothing less than Source incarnate.*

By contrast, masculine and feminine energy in their *unbalanced* states are prone to excesses. Left to its own devices, the masculine can become aggressive and potentially destructive toward others, while the feminine can be manipulative and potentially self-destructive.

Since we are emerging from an era that emphasizes doing, winning and achieving, we will naturally find more examples of excessive masculine energy.

Take corporate greed for example. It was a lightbulb moment when I realized that corporate greed is not necessarily due to "evil intent." It happens when an individual with *excessive masculine energy,* operating with no other frame of reference, becomes driven to profits at all costs. There is no real sense of "the other" and no feeling for when enough is enough. It is a relentless pursuit of "winning" and achieving.

It is not about evil. It is about imbalance. The same applies to most causes of suffering: they are caused not by evil, but by imbalance.

In *Unearthing Venus* (6) author Cate Montana writes of her interview with a South American Shaman who explains that the most important role that women play within the tribe is telling the men when to stop:

Left to their own devices, men would hunt until the last animal dies and cut down trees until there is no forest left.

What the Shaman is describing is the effect of *excessive masculine energy*.

Masculine (or feminine) energy itself is never "bad." Ever. But when it is excessive or our only frame of reference, the trouble starts.

In the tribe Montana is describing, men and women have very different, gender-specific roles. As a tribe they achieve an external kind of balance, but this is not advocated in this book. Internally each person is still in a state of imbalance because they need someone of the opposite sex to provide "opposite sex energy" and hence balance.

The new era is different. It calls upon each of us to attain balance within *ourselves*.

What are the benefits of balance?

How you can benefit

In chapter 4 we explore 10 ways being balanced will help you to thrive. To give an indication of what these are, they are presented here as questions to consider.

1. Do you yearn to be more *authentic*?
2. Do you wish to cultivate greater *happiness*?
3. Would you like a healthier *self-esteem*?
4. Do you wish for a more *balanced life*?
5. Would you like a healthy, happy and fulfilling *relationship* with your partner?

6. Do you wish to be in the flow of a *purpose-driven life*?
7. Would you like to be a more *effective leader*?
8. Do you wish to move past the societal imbalance known as *patriarchy*?
9. Would you like to cultivate a key to *Self-realization*?
10. Would you like to *co-create a better world*?

This book aims to provide a unique way of addressing these needs at their deepest source by creating the necessary balance within.

Regardless of whether you're female or male and straight, gay or trans you are on a journey of discovery toward your true nature. You are travelling a unique path. You have unique gifts to offer.

This is what thriving is all about: being yourself and truly being able to offer your gifts to the world. Being balanced does not make you the same as everyone else. We each retain our uniqueness, interests, dreams and goals. The difference is: we pursue and express these from a space of balance. This makes us far more effective.

Balance is *being who you are, just a healthier, more effective version.*

Welcome on this quintessential spiritual journey!

CHAPTER 2

What is Masculine and Feminine Energy?

What exactly is masculine and feminine energy and why is it important to know what they are?

Recently at a dinner party somebody asked:

> *Why is it important to know what is masculine energy and what is feminine energy? If a person needs to learn more empathy or assertiveness, isn't it enough just to know that?*

A reasonable question. However, as long as we remain unaware of, and disconnected from a true understanding of masculine and feminine energy, we are faced with two outcomes.

One, we will never have gender equality. Without knowing the energies, how would we come to appreciate their real value in the world? Feminine energy has been undermined during the patriarchal era. While women tend to be recognized for their nurturing and relationship-building skills – which are undoubtedly of great value, and what the world really needs now – in truth, feminine energy is much broader and extends its reach into every aspect of life.

For example, in every inspired invention made throughout history, it is actually the inventor's *feminine energy* that enabled the inventor to quiet the chattering mind, tune in and receive the inspired idea.

Elias Howe, the inventor of the sewing machine, like many inventors, received his idea during a dream. Mozart and the great composers first received the music they wrote down into a composition. Albert Einstein famously stated that imagination is more important than knowledge. These examples lie firmly in the realm of the inner feminine. This sheds light on the nature and value of feminine energy and deserves to be acknowledged and celebrated. Although women should not be equated with feminine energy, the way feminine energy is perceived and valued in the world affects gender equality. Without knowing the true value of each energy, the opposite sex will always be "other", and as a long as the masculine is in its unbalanced state, the feminine cannot shine. This is not because feminine energy is weak but because its greatness doesn't arise through battle and resistance. It arises in a supportive environment in which it is free to move and have its being.

The second outcome is we will not be able to balance ourselves.

We have been immersed in a worldview that has emphasized and elevated the masculine for the past five thousand years. Not surprisingly, we have lost touch with the feminine.

To restore feminine energy, we need to know what it represents. To understand masculine energy in its *true nature*, we need to know what it represents too. Without knowing what they are, how can we possibly embrace and bring them into balance?

We need to know, first in our minds, then in our hearts and finally in our experience, what the masculine and feminine truly are.

Clarifying the terms

What is meant by the term "energy" as in: masculine and feminine *energy*?

While some have an intuitive understanding of this term, others do not. It is a qualitative term, not a quantitative term that can be measured.

In this context "energy" is akin to "essence" – as in "feminine essence" or "masculine essence", however it is more. It is an *internal felt experience and expression* of that essence.

Tuning into your feminine energy creates a different experience than tuning into your masculine energy. The "vibe" you feel when sitting peacefully and gazing at a sunset is different from that of working relentlessly to meet a deadline. That "vibe" is the energy I am referring to, and which many of my interviewees also refer to.

To appreciate and feel enriched by the sunset, you mostly need your feminine energy. To work hard to meet your deadline, you mostly need your masculine energy.

For the scientifically-minded, one could think of masculine and feminine energy as *potential energies* that we all have access to within ourselves. The two energies can become enacted and expressed in various ways such as *kinetic energy* (which can be measured) and mental and emotional energy (which are not as measurable). By becoming balanced we are essentially freeing up potential energies that would otherwise be locked inside us. Instead, we can transform these into various kinds of activity and experience.

The terms "inner feminine", "feminine energy" and "the feminine" have the same meaning. The masculine equivalents of these are similarly interchangeable.

However, using the terms "feminine" and "masculine" can be tricky because they are loaded with connotations of biological sex. This can trick the mind into thinking "woman" when the term "feminine energy" is used, and "man" when "masculine energy" is used.

This is not the case. These energies are not gender-specific; they are universal psycho-spiritual potentialities in all of us.

Nevertheless, to avoid confusion I use a neutral term for each complementary opposite energy: I-F (Inner Feminine) and I-M (Inner Masculine).

For example:

> *John's love for animals and the environment shows that he is in touch with his I-F.*

> *Mary is developing her I-M by becoming more assertive.*

How I arrived at the definitions

For me, the meaning of I-F and I-M arose intuitively. I wanted to arrive at an unbiased understanding that plays no favorites and accurately captures the essence of each so I checked to see that my interpretations made sense.

Then I took it a step further. I realized that if *core* qualities of I-F and I-M could be identified, then any quality - empathy, assertiveness or creativity - could easily be allocated and verified as I-F or I-M without bias.

The core of each, constituting three qualities, was defined.

Defining I-F and I-M

I-F is ***inward, receptive and integrating*** (connecting).

Imagine something quintessentially feminine such as the moment of conception from a female perspective. The core qualities are fully present here.

They are also present as psycho-spiritual potentialities within every individual regardless of gender. These core I-F qualities provide the roadmap to the inner world, the heart, intuition, relationships, the big picture, the connection between things and the magic of life.

A list of 28 I-F qualities available to everyone is shown in Table 1.

As mentioned, each of these qualities can be traced to the three core qualities. This traceability is important for discerning I-F qualities from I-M qualities. This is what makes it possible to know that empathy and thinking-out-of-the-box are both I-F qualities.

Being able to trace the I-F qualities back to the three core qualities also enables us to discern *I-F,* which is available to everyone, from *stereotypical female behavior,* which is society's portrayal of the way women are expected to walk, talk, dress and behave. The latter is a human-made construct that is subject to fashion and change over time. The former is timeless and universal.

By contrast, I-M is ***outward, active*** and ***differentiating*** (setting apart).

Imagine something quintessentially masculine such as the moment of conception from a male perspective. The core qualities are fully present here.

Yet they are also present as psycho-spiritual potentialities within every individual regardless of gender. These core I-M qualities provide the map to the outer world, the head, logical reasoning, focus, tasks, discerning differences and creating structure.

The list of 28 I-M qualities available to everyone is shown in Table 1.

All the I-M qualities can be traced to the three core qualities. This traceability makes it possible to know that determination and linear thinking are both I-M qualities.

Being able to trace the I-M qualities back to the three core qualities enables us to discern *I-M,* which is available to everyone, from *stereotypical male behavior,* which is a macho image of the way men are expected to walk, talk, dress and behave.

The former is timeless and universal. The latter is a human-made construct and is subject to change. Consider the tunics worn by Roman soldiers 2000 years ago, which are no longer considered ideal clothing for men in battle.

Although the qualities in Table 1 are *universally available* to men and women, not every individual has *integrated and enlivened* these qualities.

Yet, regardless of which qualities have been enlivened in us, all of these qualities *belong* to all of us. It is a human right that we can access and express these.

How does it feel to know that every one of these capabilities is available to you?

Table 1: I-F and I-M qualities available to everyone

	I-F	I-M
Core	Inward, receptive, integrating	Outward, active, differentiating
Qualities	Self-awareness Influencing self Personal growth Awareness of the subtle and transcendent/spiritual Tuning in to your purpose Surrendering and letting go Attracting desired outcomes through intentionality Ability to step back/rest/play Intuition/gut feelings Ability to listen/read others Heart/empathizing We/collectivism Collaboration/team work Synthesis/commonality Ability to integrate People-focus Coaching and empowering Transformational leadership Sustainability/greater good Big picture view Patterns and trends Creativity Thinking out-of-the-box Long-term view Wider implications Equality Commonality Flexibility and flow	Self-expression Influencing others Outer achievements Attention on external, physical reality Taking action to get there Determination and hard work Attaining desired outcomes through effort and action Ability to focus/work Logic/linear thinking Ability to assert/self-express Head/understanding Me/individuality Self-reliance/individual work Analysis/difference Ability to differentiate Task-focus Mentoring and advising Transactional leadership Profit/my success Detailed, focused view Data and information Precision Structured thinking Short-term view Immediate implications Hierarchy Difference Rules and structure

Table 1 is not intended to be a comprehensive list but serves as a frame of reference for I-F and I-M qualities.

Everyday examples of I-F and I-M

What does I-F look like in everyday situations? Here are some examples to consider in your life.

- Intuition and the ability to receive spiritual guidance
- Having a sudden flash of insight "out of the blue"
- Utilising the Law of Attraction to attain your goals and dreams
- Having a heartfelt connection with another human being
- Having love, respect and connection with animals and the environment
- The ability to care for and nurture others
- Inclusiveness and empathy for others
- Seeking win-win solutions
- Leading with passion, humility and higher purpose
- Harnessing the power of teams or groups through collaboration
- Creativity and thinking out of the box
- Making considered decisions by factoring in the complexities
- Mediating conflict by acknowledging several points of view
- Caring about those less fortunate
- Picking up on subtle cues in a conversation
- Being a listening ear
- Taking a break or stepping back to survey your work
- Empowering others to find their solutions
- Feeling the awe and mystery of life
- Absorbing the beauty of a sunrise or sunset
- Being present in the moment
- Being happy for no external reason
- The ability to be playful

Conversely, what does I-M look like in everyday situations? Here are some examples to consider in your own life:

- Taking action to make your dreams come true
- Determination and perseverance to get the job done
- Figuring out how to fix something
- Mastering the art of self-reliance
- Standing up for yourself
- Being willing to assert your needs
- Enjoying competition
- Expressing yourself externally in the world via your career/work
- The ability to earn money
- Leading with a focus on tasks, deadlines and completion
- Focusing on tangible, measurable outcomes
- Creating the conditions to ensure profitability in business
- The art of mentoring and skill-building
- Creating structure, order, processes and policies
- Ensuring rules are adhered to
- Respect for hierarchy
- Making quick decisions by considering immediate inputs
- Taking executive decisions to prevent gridlock
- Creating new technologies
- Striving for efficiency, precision, accuracy and quality
- Cultivating self-discipline
- The ability to take risks

Here is an example of someone who embodies balance.

A man ahead of his time

As a college student in the early 1990s I was intrigued by a certain professor whom I will call "Prof Brown". He was a Professor Emeritus, head of the Geology Department and Dean of Science. There was something special about him though at the time I couldn't articulate it.

Already probably in his late fifties at that time, he was successful by outward standards, given his high standing at the university. But there was more to him. He exuded happiness in his being. It seemed to be the kind that exists regardless of outer circumstances – an I-F quality.

As a teacher he easily commanded the attention in the room. His presence was powerful, yet his passion and love for the subject shone through. Lectures were often punctuated by fun or mischief that he generated. For him work seemed also to be play.

Geology field trips were notorious for students getting out of hand and partying a little too hard. During one particular field trip a first-year student, perhaps eager to impress, had partied particularly hard the night before. The next morning as students gathered to hear information about the local geology, this student managed to fall asleep on his feet. Initially swaying a little, he then keeled right over, falling face down into a soft pile of mud. The next thing I saw was Prof Brown arched backwards with laughter. The partying wasn't mentioned once; there was no need.

In class he drummed in the need to make presentations colorful and attractive. This was unusual in the field of science, in a time where technical precision was of utmost importance and aesthetics were almost considered inconsequential. He had an eye for both.

Prof Brown was locally famous for his hobby of building large and beautiful kites with innovative designs. He published a book about it, a labor of love that he had shared with his then 12-year-old daughter. She was depicted in the book flying various kite models.

To me he was a real **mensch**. *A multi-faceted person. He was strong, yet gentle and kind; accomplished, yet humble and self-effacing; analytical and serious, yet lighthearted and even silly at times. He took his work seriously, yet it never took on a mantle of "heaviness". He made time for family and for his passion of building kites. Clearly, he maintained a healthy work-life balance. His easy-go-lucky manner, quiet confidence and keen sense of humor seemed to draw to him whatever he needed, without struggle.*

Many people might describe such as person as a *mensch* or someone with that elusive "x-factor." Those are good descriptions, but as an explanation he was balanced: he exuded a healthy balance of I-M and I-F.

I-F and I-M in partnership

The first step to balance is getting to know our I-F and I-M so that we can begin to integrate them into our being. Yet, being balanced is not merely a static situation with both sides enlivened; it is a dance between the two.

While this could play out in many ways, it is helpful to know that there is an essential way that these two complementary opposites work together in partnership: your I-F brings higher purpose, direction and sustainability to the drive and energy generated by your I-M.

This is how you would, for example, live a purpose-driven life: taking inspired action. Inspired (I-F) action (I-M).

Therefore, I-F is our compass. It guides our actions toward positive, mutually beneficial and sustainable outcomes. It enables us to achieve our goals while sustaining the planet and the health and wellbeing of all. It also enables us to flow with life and attract to us the things we most want through synchronicities.

I-F is no less than our connection to the Divine. Only the I-F can intuit and receive the guidance that imbues our actions (I-M) with meaning and purpose, enabling us to be in the flow of life.

If I-F is the compass, I-M is in a word, action. I-M enables us to get the job done efficiently and to a high standard. This is borne of an ability to handle technical detail and precision as well as an inherent drive for action and reaping the satisfaction of a project completed.

However, with excessive I-M unbalanced by I-F, we would be "all action, no direction", a recipe for working relentlessly or taking action for its own sake, and without considering the impacts on others or the planet.

Here is an excerpt from the story of Paulo, the business entrepreneur (chapter 9).

> *One of the prices I paid in having that black-and-white mentality is that in a lot of cases it puts the onus for life and success and responsibility purely 100% on you.*
>
> *It's as if the only person who can shape your destiny is you. And I've now learned that that is not entirely true. I think that is half the picture. You certainly initiate it and get it going but then life and people will come and collude with you and it'll happen if you let it. Whereas when you were in black-and-white mode, everything was up to you. Once I began to tap the other side of the energy I started to allow things to happen that I wouldn't ordinarily have and they would turn out really well for me. And I would think "wow, I would never have gone there on my own."*

With excessive I-F unbalanced by I-M, we might have great and noble ideas, but unable to bring them into fruition.

One begins to get a sense of how fruitful life can be when the I-F and I-M operate in their most natural state - in collaboration and partnership. With these complementary opposite energies enlivened and brought into partnership, life becomes imbued with magic.

This is being in the flow of life, where we are guided, where synchronicities happen and we find ourselves in the right place at the right time in order to take the next step.

Rather than being the opposing forces they're often made out to be, I-F and I-M are true partners. When they operate together, they have the potential to bring heaven on earth.

Questions you can ask yourself

- Which side do you tend to resonate with more: I-F or I-M?
- What is the outcome of this approach?
- Which I-F or I-M qualities do you excel at?
- Which qualities would you like to enhance?

Guided meditation: meet your Inner Masculine and Feminine

The following guided meditation will help you to visualize and develop a personal relationship with your I-F and I-M. What follows is a shortened version of a powerful guided meditation I experienced while attending a course offered by Heather Linn, a spiritual healer and teacher.

I suggest you set aside 15 minutes or more. You could ask a friend to read this to you or you could pre-record your own voice and then do the exercise.

1. Get into a comfortable lying down position and close your eyes.
2. Allow yourself to relax (you could use a favorite relaxation technique or breathing practice)
3. Imagine you are in a beautiful setting – perhaps a forest, a beach or a garden – whatever feels comfortable to you. You are sitting comfortably, feeling the peace and serenity of the environment.
4. While you are relaxing, you call forth your masculine energy to appear in form. It takes the form of a man and slowly walks toward you. He stops and respectfully stands nearby. See him entering the scene. Notice what he is wearing. Notice his features. Look into his eyes. Feel the energy radiating from him. What message does he convey to you?
5. Now you call forth your feminine energy to appear in form. This takes the form of woman and slowly walks toward you. She stops and respectfully stands nearby. See her entering the scene. Notice what she is wearing. Notice her features. Look into her eyes. Feel the energy radiating from her. What message does she convey to you?
6. Ask your masculine and feminine energies to turn to each other now. How do they relate to each other? Are they standing near each other or further away now? Are they looking at one another or away from each other? What energy are they emitting as they do this?
7. What are her needs? Listen as she speaks to him. What are his needs? Hear him as he speaks to her. Give yourself time and

listen as the two figures communicate with each other. You may not hear specific messages but you may sense how they relate to one another. Welcome their communication and send love and appreciation to each of these two aspects of yourself. Does this feel complete or is there something you wish to ask them to do differently in the future?
8. When the encounter feels complete welcome your I-M and I-F into your being. Allow them to take up space in your being. When you are ready slowly come out and open your eyes.

What did you glean from this encounter? You may want to write down any messages or insights that arose.

CHAPTER 3

My Balancing Act

My journey to balance was not predictable.

Since I am a female, it might be reasonable to assume that my greatest challenge was integrating my I-M. This was not the case for me, and interestingly, not for most of the women interviewed for this book. It seems that I-F is something we all have to learn to integrate.

One of the keys to integrating my I-F was discerning the *true feminine* from *socialized expectations of women*.

I needed to find a way to be proud of what I-F represented. Yet, in the context of living in a patriarchal society that devalues the feminine, this was no small challenge.

It took years to get to the point where I recognized I-F for what it is but when that point came, the integration process was quick. There was nothing to resist but instead, much to look forward to. I saw dramatic and positive changes.

How did I get to that point?

From the age of four, I had the feeling my life would be unconventional.

I played and had fun like many kids do, but I was a deep thinker. I wanted more than to marry, have kids and go through the same challenges that seemed to occur with women around me and in previous generations.

I wanted to know what was really going on, what life was all about.

Specifically, I wanted to know: who am I? Who is God/Spirit/Source? How do we relate to it? Why are we here? *Within* that larger, spiritual understanding: what is gender? Why is there a battle of the sexes? Why do women seem so burdened? What can we do to restore peace and harmony?

During my teenage years and beyond, I derived insights into these mysteries by studying Eastern spirituality, Western mysticism and near-death experiences. I took on board what felt right. This wasn't hard to do because much of what I was learning felt familiar and kindled traces of my own distant memory. Despite my Catholic upbringing, I felt instinctively that reincarnation was real. It felt normal, almost mundane to me.

Spiritual experience

As though to support my desire for a deeper understanding, I had a life-altering spiritual experience at the age of six.

> *While gazing intensely at a book, I suddenly find myself in outer space. I see the Earth and moon from a distance, and many stars against the deep blackness. I am not afraid - I am awe-struck by the deep, resonant silence. It and the sense of deep space are breathtaking. It is awesome, yet somehow familiar.*
>
> *After basking in this experience for a while, I suddenly find myself in a different location, as though ushered there by some unseen intelligence operating behind the scenes. This time I find myself gazing at two planets, one circling the other.*
>
> *Then I notice something unexpected: each planet is conscious. In some way that I cannot explain, I am able to "see" into their soul. Each has an intact sense of self-awareness and a keen awareness of the other. Their circling motion is not just a mechanical phenomenon; it is a joyful dance. The gravitational force between them is itself alive with intelligence and a tingly sensation.*

The message I received was: The universe is conscious; there is more to life than surface appearances.

Looking back, this experience gave me the beginnings of a new perspective on life. This would enable me to look deeper, even when it came to such things as patriarchy and the suppression of the feminine.

Enjoying both sides as a youngster

As a youngster I enjoyed a lot of freedom. Although growing up in a conservative neighborhood during apartheid-era South Africa, my parents had a rather *laissez-faire* approach to raising my two brothers and me.

I became an all-rounder. On the one hand, I loved sports, climbing trees, adventure and travel. From a young age I had an aptitude for math, science and spatial abilities. Since the age of 10, I would take the bus on my own and travel into the city, browse the shops and have fun, learn to find my way around, then take the bus back. Little did I know how much this would help me in later years when I travelled the world.

On the other hand, I loved the gentler pursuits such as art, music, reading, playing with my dog, hanging out with friends, baking cupcakes with my mother or just being among the flowers and trees in the garden. I had a good dose of both kinds of experiences.

Unlike most of my friends, who over the years seemed more willing to give up pursuits that were deemed "for the opposite sex", I was not.

As I approached my teens the pressure to conform and "be like other girls" grew rapidly. The "in-crowd" seemed to be those who went along with the peer pressure. The more girls and boys conformed to it, the more popular they seemed to be. I, on the other hand, happily remained a tomboy.

When I saw the posturing and airs girls put on just to impress boys, I felt uncomfortable. It seemed fake and somewhat manipulative. Was that really what the feminine represented, I wondered?

I yearned to know a version of the feminine that felt positive, affirming and empowering. I did not like what society offered as its version of the feminine.

Relationship with the feminine goes south

My first impressions of the feminine left me confused. It seemed to have a bad name.

It was not associated with strength or substance. When I looked around I saw it depicted as posturing behavior bolstered with lipstick, short skirts, make-up and high heels. I tried it out. Just to see. I went to the movies with my first boyfriend, Mark (a relationship that lasted two whole weeks) but it did not sit well - literally. Rather than being able to relax and be myself, I found myself constantly having to watch how I was sitting. I pressed my knees together and kept monitoring lest my undies show at any time.

What a colossal waste of time and energy, I thought. Surely my scintillating conversation would be enough? Wearing these things was fine for special occasions but every day, as part of the daily me? Err, no thanks.

My second sense around the feminine was that of a deep but often unexpressed sadness. As a young girl I became aware of sexism and the limiting roles it afforded to women.

My grandmother was a walking example of this saddened I-F. A gentle and intuitive soul, she raised six children with a husband who was anything but hands-on with the children. She seemed worn out by life and old before her time. It affected me to see her that way. Yet, she wasn't the only one. Other women in my mother's generation seemed embittered, not merely resigned to their lot in life.

I wanted women to be happy, to feel fulfilled, to be able to realize their dreams.

The third sense I had of the feminine was that it was depicted as "the loser in a man's world."

This gave me a sense of humiliation around femininity and being female. Who wants to be associated with being a loser? While outwardly I stood up for women, inwardly I was confused by the image of weakness and oppression that society seemed to present as "the feminine."

I sensed that this was not really the feminine. I knew she existed somewhere in the recesses of our collective psyche and in my own. It would take me another fifteen years to find her.

Rebelling and claiming my masculine side

Enter the rebellion phase.

Within the context of a world that seemed to value the masculine over the feminine, I began to dissociate from the feminine within myself. Gradually I began to see femininity – at least the *societal version of it* - as not worth pursuing.

So I began to lean toward my masculine side. It felt like the safe choice given that this was what the world seemed to value more.

Unknowingly I began to foster a mindset later identified as "internalized patriarchy." This occurs when a woman unwittingly exerts the same biases against the feminine that patriarchy does.

Internalized patriarchy tends to play out in one of two ways, and to greater or lesser degrees.

The first: a woman connects to her masculine side. She may use this fiery energy to rebel against patriarchy and to stand up for other women. Yet, she is really only standing up for the masculine side of women – for their independence and freedom to express themselves outside the domestic sphere. She finds certain aspects of the feminine - their softer, nurturing qualities - problematic. She has in effect bought into the paradigm by dismissing the feminine and joining the ranks of men in an attempt to feel equal.

In the second option, a woman connects to her feminine side, albeit the submissive version advocated by a patriarchal society. She gives her power away to her "knight in shining armor" who is expected to take her problems away and support her because she is so delicate. She projects her I-M onto her partner, becoming the feminine half of the gender binary. She has in effect bought into the paradigm by surrendering to its "reality" and identifying with the conditioned female role within it.

Both kinds of internalized patriarchy can be very subtle, hard to notice at all. It took a great deal of self-awareness for me to see it. In my case, it was the first type. I stood up for women's rights but I simultaneously felt upset with women for letting themselves get into this situation and I felt uncomfortable with aspects of femininity, and the sense of vulnerability it led to.

One of the outcomes of internalized patriarchy is a tendency to place men and I-M on a pedestal. This could play out in different ways: automatically conferring more authority to a man's viewpoint during a conversation or habitually fussing over men, to name just two examples.

Ever seen a group of women chatting happily together, yet when a man walks into the room the conversation is dropped like a hot potato and the attention quickly moves to him?

Another way in which internalized patriarchy subtly plays out is when women downplay other women's abilities or achievements. Several years ago I was shocked to hear a friend and successful businesswoman say: "I wouldn't want to fly in an airplane with a female pilot."

Internalized patriarchy plays out differently in different people. We all unwittingly participate in it until we consciously remove ourselves from it.

How else could it have been? We were raised in a paradigm and this affects us at a sub-conscious level. It is only natural that there is some unlearning to do.

Nevertheless, at that time I had not heard of internalized patriarchy and did not recognize my own thinking for what it was. I was a confused, upset teenager. As a result, I entered a twelve-year period in which I was a lot more in touch with my masculine side.

Exploring and developing my masculine side

In high school when many girls became ever more "girly" and began to step back from math and science, I excelled in them. A career counsellor said: "Loraine, you can do anything you put your mind to, but you are particularly suited to architecture, science or engineering." I studied science and became a hydrogeologist.

During this masculine phase, I had a variety of interesting relationships. I got along easily with guys, especially the intellectual ones. My first boyfriend was one of those; we met in the chess team. He also happened to be tall, dark and handsome.

With a four-year age gap between us I began to enjoy being with a boyfriend who was older. I have had three significant relationships with older men. Each man had an intriguing mixture of I-M and I-F. Each one of my partners was active and sporty, a leader of sorts in his community. Yet each one was a gentle soul with a love of nature and people. Each was unique in his own way and did not fit into a male stereotype. I loved that. I was drawn to men who were already accomplished in some way, and for whom I was no threat. Men who felt free to be themselves and let me be free to be myself.

Like the men I preferred to date, my younger brother Michael also embodied a blend of I-M and I-F. A competitive, sporty, intelligent soul, he had already delved into self-awareness and personal growth by the time he was in high school.

My world was rocked when he died in a car accident at the age of 19.

We were just beginning to become true friends when this happened. His passing was to become a major catalyst for my spiritual growth. I had always been drawn to esoteric, spiritual and alternative thinking. But now it was catapulted to a new level. Through incredible synchronistic events I came across an Eastern spiritual path and was drawn to it like a homesick child. I became a vegetarian and began to meditate.

This brought my I-F back into the picture.

It started a process of me returning to myself, my inner world, the subtle, feelings, the spiritual. It sowed a seed but the pressures of studies and working life kept it from fully germinating for another ten years.

I was first to explore my masculine side to its full extent before returning to balance and bringing the softer side into fruition.

After graduating I began my first career in a prominent consulting engineering company. Within a year I was caught up in the drive for results and success. I began to work 60 – 70 hour weeks, often coming in to work over weekends. The promotions came in fast. Soon I was the youngest and first female manager in the firm's then 25-year history.

Life was a drive for success. Working long hours and weekends meant that I could finish projects on time and churn them out faster than anyone could say "New York minute."

I began to realize "Hey, I can *do* things!"

I could solve problems and make things happen, which created a newfound sense of self-confidence. It felt good to be in control, like I was on top of things.

This relentless activity was to come at a cost, but that would only emerge a little later.

My assertive, masculine side benefited me in many ways.

When I was offered a position at the consulting engineering firm I rejected their initial salary offer - not that I had the faintest clue whether it was a reasonable salary or not. As a graduate student I didn't know, plus the Internet wasn't around in those days. Nevertheless, I'd assumed this was how things were done and it paid off. I got a better offer.

One day, after a few years of work experience, I asked my manager (whom I trusted implicitly): "How do I know that I'm not being paid less just because I'm a woman"?

He said he'd look into it. A couple of days later he came back, "Loraine, you are the highest paid of anyone in your category in this firm." I was good with that.

After a few years my drive for achievement started to take its toll. I began to run out of steam.

There were several warning signs. That I had become a workaholic was one. During one particular year I took three weekends off. The rest of the year was just work, work, work.

My eating habits were typical of a high flyer: I skipped breakfast every day and lived on TV dinners. I went jogging six days a week as a way of relaxing. Sure, jogging releases stress but this was just another form of "work hard, play hard."

I am sharing this information to paint a picture of what it can look like to operate from excessive I-M.

One day I realized that I was trembling and I went to see a doctor. He informed me that I was not eating enough (due to skipping meals) and that my body was showing signs of starting to digest itself. A flashing red light. There was more to come.

There was my relationship. I was in a challenging relationship with Anthony. He was a kind-hearted, but rather aloof and somewhat troubled personality who had a hard time showing his emotions.

When we met I felt: "I know this person." His energy felt familiar and comfortable. He was an attractive man with a toned, athletic body and kind eyes. He was in some ways the product of a strict English upbringing, where emotions were frowned upon and feelings were best kept to oneself.

Yet I loved him and I wanted our relationship to work more than anything. When things didn't seem to work easily for us I fell into bouts of depression.

I had given my power away: I had allowed my wellbeing to be entirely dependent on how warm and available he was to me. This fluctuated quite a bit. One day, my intuition spoke clearly. We were on vacation but rather than having a wonderful time we were arguing. That day I got a urinary tract infection, my sign for when things are really out of balance.

That night I was taken to hospital. The doctor confirmed that he had never seen such a bad case before. My intuition said: "Time to move on from this relationship!"

Then a final wake-up call: I went to see a therapist to work through my relationship issues.

She asked a simple question, but one that left me utterly stumped: "How are you feeling right now?"

I must have looked like I'd seen a ghost. I stammered as I struggled to find the words. I couldn't access my feelings. I tried *thinking* about how I was feeling, but it wasn't the same thing. *This* is how far I had gotten out of touch myself, my I-F.

Then a positive sign came. I had dreamed of taking a year off to travel overseas and was discussing this with a friend, Peter, who challenged me, "If you are going to wait for someone else to go with you, you'll never go. Just go by yourself."

A door flung open in my mind. Thank you, Peter! After that everything fell into place within a few short months.

At the age of 29 I had hit the maximum levels of imbalance toward the I-M. Outwardly I was successful and accomplished. I was earning excellent money and had paid off all my debts. I was well on my way to becoming the youngest - and only second - female director in the firm's history.

But I was exhausted, less than happy and out of touch with myself.

Joy was not something I could easily tune into: I was too busy to stop long enough to let it in, to feel it.

One exception to all this was my cat, Samson, my cherished companion and my first experience of unconditional love in this lifetime.

Clearly this was a very masculine phase of my life. Even so, there were exceptions that represented I-F.

One major exception was the impact of the loss of my younger brother and the spiritual growth it fostered. Another exception was my relationship with Anthony: rather than being in my I-M with him, I had adopted an immature I-F, a tendency to give my power away to make the relationship work even at the cost of my own wellbeing. My meditation, my love of music, chocolate and my cat – these were all doorways to the feminine.

Yet despite these, on the whole my life was dominated by I-M.

By the time I was 29 I had deeply explored my I-M and discovered much about what it had to offer. Clearly it had a lot to offer! But too much of it led me to lose a vital aspect of myself. At this point I wanted more than anything to come back to the deeper aspects of myself. To experience balance.

Thus, I left my job and my relationship, and sold everything I had in order to take a year off and travel the world.

I would go in search of myself, of a new life and a new career that felt more aligned with my purpose.

Re-awakening the feminine

My year of travel was balm for the soul. Suddenly I had the luxury of time. Time to reflect, read, heal and just be. I could breathe again. I spent many happy hours in cafes all over the world devouring spiritual and self-help books while journaling with a cappuccino at hand.

Part of my travels entailed a trip to California to visit friends and family. I say "family" because I had been fortunate enough to spend a year with an American family in Southern California as an exchange student during my senior year of high school. They had become my adopted American family.

While in the US I unexpectedly came across a three-year study program that was to change my life. It was an MA in Consciousness

Studies at John F. Kennedy University in the San Francisco Bay Area. A psychic in Hawaii had suggested that I visit the university just to check it out. The moment I stepped onto the campus my entire body lit up with goose bumps. I knew I had to be there.

It turned out to be the best thing I have ever done for myself – aside from my marriage a few years later.

Imagine the effect of being in a progressive college program that is experiential rather than purely academic, and focuses on consciousness, spiritual modalities, emotional intelligence, positive psychology, transpersonal psychology, Eastern philosophy, indigenous wisdom, women's studies and human potential.

It was like being in a spiritual candy store.

Students were mostly in their thirties, forties and fifties - women and men with loads of life experience and wisdom. It was like coming home, the closest thing to "heaven on earth." Many times while riding the train home after a class, my body would be covered in goose bumps as I reflected on what I had discovered in class that day. Many times it felt like the lectures were channeled; such pure, essential and nourishing knowledge.

This experiential program brought me back to myself and my I-F.

Here I'm talking about the *true feminine*.

Three years later, after graduating from the program I was a transformed person.

What was different? I was back in touch with myself. I was comfortable with having feelings and knew how to allow them to be without judgment or fear. I had healed a lot of pain from my past by acknowledging it and allowing myself to move through it "with no blame or shame."

This is a method for getting to the source of a problem by discovering the original limiting belief that gave rise to it. I knew how to manage my feelings so that I could dissipate them and feel better whenever needed.

I tuned into my feelings easily, even the subtle ones.

I developed a newfound sense of compassion for myself. This made it easier to connect with others. I learned to be comfortable with other people's emotions without being overwhelmed by them or trying to fix the situation. I could be with others and "just be" together.

What a shift from my previous mindset!

I had developed a newfound respect and appreciation for women and I-F. I was surrounded by incredible female role models - professors, colleagues and friends. Their personal power, wisdom and compassion shone through. They were making the world a better place through their work and in their being. These women were unique individuals, some with more than a touch of eccentricity. They were whole human beings.

Similarly, I met men who were bold and impressive, yet unapologetically in touch with their feminine side, similarly making the world a better place in their own ways.

I reconnected with my intuition in powerful ways. I experienced a series of 12 after-death communications with my younger brother in the form of dreams. A new relationship opened up between us; to this day it is a source of joy.

My psychic faculties started opening up. During an energy healing session I looked down and saw my heart chakra as clear as day. I could see it, feel it and hear it.

I received inner guidance and nature support. By "nature support" I mean the opportunities, synchronicities and unexpected gifts that arise from being in the flow of life. Whatever I needed would somehow be taken care of. For example, I needed to create income to support every aspect of my life including my study fees. As a foreign student I was not permitted to work, other than part-time on campus. This was insufficient to meet my financial needs.

I began a pet-sitting business on the side. It got off to a good start but I needed more business. Within a short time, an established pet-sitter with a whole book of business in the San Francisco Bay Area left her entire clientele to me when she moved to a different state. We had only met a couple of times.

I was beginning to attract desired outcomes, rather than the usual way of hard work and struggle. To me this was another sign of the feminine magic returning.

Eventually I left the US once my student visa ran out, returned to South Africa and entered the corporate world. It was really hard to leave behind the world I felt was my home.

Nevertheless, I got an unusual job that softened the blow. I was a *cultural liaison* working between the US and South African offices of an international financial services firm. This was a big change from my previous career as it was all about people and relationships. Looking back, I generally did well. Not perfectly, but well. My work, which involved cross-cultural and soft skills training, morphed over time and I became the training manager. I worked with people ranging from the CEO to all levels of the company and across cultures.

As though to confirm how much more balanced I'd become as a person, I was required to take a cognitive assessment to find out how my brain works and how well I'd potentially fit with the job.

The results showed that my brain was entirely balanced. It showed equal-sized circles depicting the use of logic/analytical thinking on the one hand and intuitive/emotional awareness on the other hand.

The industrial psychologist said emphatically: "I seldom see this. Most people lean strongly one way or the other, but you have both." Given my life's journey, this was not totally surprising, but it was a nice validation.

Seventeen years' prior, the tests I took for a career advisor showed very different results. After all, she had said "You are particularly suited to architecture, engineering and science."

Getting to know the true feminine

One of my greatest insights has been the discovery of the *true feminine*.

It is not about "acting girly" or wearing certain clothes.

If women wanted to do that, fine, but I discovered those things weren't essential for being in touch with my I-F. This is important because many people would not be comfortable integrating their I-F if it meant having to walk, talk and dress in a certain way. How would men ever integrate their I-F?

The point is: there is a difference between the true feminine and the socialized feminine image. The true feminine is available to everyone.

This distinction was illumined by Ruth, an older woman whom I had known most of my life. Ruth had mastered her socialized feminine image, but died in her seventies not having embodied as much of the true feminine.

Ruth lived her life according to societal expectations in terms of dress code, manner and style. She behaved as someone with the second type of internalized patriarchy discussed earlier which entails adhering to gender stereotypical behavior. She refused to learn to drive a car because she believed that it was "a man's job" and that driving was "unfeminine."

Physically, Ruth was very attractive. As a young woman she could have been a Hollywood star. Every time I saw her she looked elegant in a dress with coiffed hair and make-up. She had four children and had been a teacher before but never worked in a job after marrying. Although she loved her children she was never one to show her affection easily. Her husband was a shy, soft-spoken, slightly aloof man.

Ruth started drinking and battled with alcoholism for most of her adult life. It got worse. Much later in life she developed shingles and skin issues. She seemed frustrated by life, and dare I say, unfulfilled. She had never allowed herself to pursue interests outside of her role as wife and stay-at-home mom.

While those provided a sense of fulfilment up to a point, she clearly needed more, especially when the children were older and out of the house.

The I-F – being in touch with our inner world, our intuition, our feelings, our ability to nurture and our sense of purpose – is absolutely necessary for living a fulfilling life. How else would we tune into ourselves and receive guidance? How else would we connect emotionally with others? How would we tune into the joys of life?

Observing Ruth over the decades showed me how imperative it is to understand this difference. Many women are preoccupied with conforming to a socialized feminine image – having been raised to believe that this is the only way for a woman to be - and yet remain largely unaware of the true feminine.

Once I understood this distinction, life again became simpler and more beautiful.

What a discovery: I could be myself and wear things that are comfortable to me; walk and talk the way I want to and yet fully develop my I-F.

True freedom. Utter bliss.

I wanted to kiss and embrace the feminine for all her beauty, intelligence and value. This is what I had been yearning for all along.

Living from a space of balance

Life is vastly richer for having become more balanced.

During my late thirties I met and married Simon, who is also my best friend and soul mate.

Being married to a balanced person (my husband) has revealed the beauty that relationships are capable of. We have many touchpoints from which to connect and share experiences. These include meditation, working from home, cycling, surfing, traveling, scooter rides, DIY projects, cooking, theatre and myriad other ways to have fun. We sometimes even meet to go shopping together as a fun event.

We are guided by Ayurveda and other natural health principles for healthy eating and a balanced lifestyle.

Today we live in our dream home that I believe we manifested more through intentionality than hard work. We live here with our two cats, a lovely garden, bicycles and surfboards. (When I come back in a future life I want to come back as one of my cats. They have a great life.)

My work has evolved over the years into corporate coaching, with some lecturing and public speaking. It keeps me busy and is highly fulfilling. Yet I also love to garden and have developed a hobby as an artist.

While I am proud of the achievements of my twenties as a young professional who mostly operated from her I-M, I am thrilled to have gone beyond that. Life is so much richer and happier with inner balance leading the way.

CHAPTER 4

Ten Benefits of Balance

"How will I benefit from being balanced?"

There are probably too many ways to count, however, this chapter outlines 10 major benefits of balance. These can be thought of as the outcomes that arise due to the *Law of Balance*.

Depending on how far you progress toward inner balance, these will enable you to thrive in the most important areas of your life.

1. Authenticity

Authenticity is being true to yourself and giving expression to that which is you. This requires sufficient self-awareness to be guided by the inner compass (I-F) and the courage to express yourself accordingly (I-M).

Yet, as a result of conditioning, most people tend to identify with one *or* the other side of themselves. When life presents itself in its myriad expressions and diverse moments many people have a limited range of responses available to them.

Being authentic means being able to choose from within the entire "toolkit" of I-M and I-F qualities and either respond to, or create, what is actually needed in the moment.

Paulo, who we briefly met in chapter 1, illustrates this:

> *As a child, if I did anything that was considered feminine, the guys would make fun of me. Once I discovered that I legitimately have two sides to me, I made peace with it. I thought: "Make all the fun you want, it's quite OK, I know why I'm doing this." I think as a result I began to express myself better. I think the world began to see a more authentic me than the one that existed before.*
>
> *The one that existed before - every time it did something it was going through a social checklist to make sure that it could tick the boxes and it wasn't going to get criticism.*

Being authentic requires us to get past the social checklist. It is about being true to ourselves and not being limited to conditioned responses.

Evidence shows that this freedom is exceptionally rare. According to Bronnie Ware, author of *The Top Five Regrets of the Dying* (7), the single-most common regret of the dying is:

> *I wish I'd had the courage to live a life true to myself, not the life others expected of me.*

Ware reports that many of her patients had not honored even half the dreams and hopes they had once cherished.

Being balanced affords us the freedom to let go of what other people might think so that we can be authentic.

2. Happiness

There is more than one way to experience happiness.

One is achieving something you have worked hard for. This is the I-M route.

When I was heavily engaged with my career as a hydrogeologist this kind of happiness was available to me every time I completed a project. Given my workaholic tendencies, it happened quite often. This was the reward that I was willing to work nights and weekends for. The joy of achievement. It was palpable; and it kept me coming back for more.

Then I noticed something about this experience of happiness: it was intense, but short-lived. What about all the time spent between those highs?

Fortunately, there are more ways.

Another way, which I only realized later, is cultivating a "background happiness." This is "happiness for no reason" and it represents the I-F route to happiness using awareness, feelings and intention.

It is a state of being independent of outer circumstances. The amazing thing is that it can be cultivated to be there all the time, even in difficult situations.

As a child I heard a radio show in which a guest speaker announced that it is possible to be happy in all circumstances, even at a funeral. I was intrigued. I knew it was true; I just didn't know how to cultivate it. Fortunately, there are now entire books dedicated to the subject. In essence it requires I-F: surrendering, letting go of control, setting aside judgment, cultivating self-acceptance, self-love, acceptance of what is, allowing and being open to receive. This kind of happiness is always available to us; it is a question of allowing it in.

Rafaella, a 38-year old spiritual seeker, teacher and mother, describes her levels of happiness since she became more balanced.

> *I have a lot more happiness now than in the part of my life when I was much more in my masculine side. I had happiness then but it was another kind of happiness. I got happiness from my interaction with the world but it was more fleeting and perhaps a bit more superficial. My happiness now feels more grounded. There is a feeling of trust that is present now. Sometimes life can be difficult but now I can respond more consciously. Previously when life was hard it felt like the end of the world to me.*

Rafaella had previously experienced the I-M route to happiness that comes through career and interactions with the world, but she describes it as a fleeting kind of happiness. At that point in her life she didn't feel she was in the right career, which could have added to the fleeting nature of her happiness then. However, after several years of self-discovery, getting onto her spiritual path and having children, Rafaella experienced a lot of her I-F. This brought her in touch with the second kind of happiness described earlier.

I-M and I-F bring different routes to, and experiences of, happiness. A third experience of happiness comes from the dynamics of balance: where I-M works in conjunction with I-F as nature intended. This means *doing what you love* and taking steps in the direction of your dreams.

Here's how Rafaella describes her experience since becoming more balanced:

> *Since I've taken responsibility for my life I can no longer be a victim. When you take responsibility and you find your power you have to move with that and reach for what you want. To be connected and to feel this integration between I-F and I-M energies: that is happiness.*

I was nearly 40 when I took up surfing, something I had been dreaming of since being a teenager. I tried it then but it got shelved as I became an adult and life happened. More than 20 years later, it became possible again when my husband and I moved to the ocean.

Being nearly 40 at the time, I could have dismissed it as an idea belonging to my youth. I could have worried about what others might think. But I chose to follow my heart instead. Surfing is now one of my favorite activities. Nothing compares to the sheer bliss and sense of rejuvenation it brings. I feel months younger after a surfing session. The best part is my husband took up surfing alongside me, adding even more to the joy because now it is shared. As the saying goes: "shared joy is a double joy."

There are more ways than one to experience happiness. Balance is the secret.

3. Self-esteem

Christine Arylo, author of *Madly in Love with ME* (2012) defines self-esteem as:

> *A strong belief in and regard for yourself. A strong confidence in your ability to do and be anything.*

As a hydrogeologist in my twenties, I became aware of innate capabilities that related to my I-M. The challenges that needed to be overcome in my line of work helped me to see that I could do things. These were newly-realized capabilities.

My job involved a mixture of field work and office work. While out in the field supervising drillers and other contractors we would more than occasionally run into problems that I was ultimately responsible for solving. These could vary from a drilling rig struggling to penetrate a hard layer of rock to having equipment fail while we were out in the sticks, or other logistical or budgetary issues. Yet I solved them.

In the office I ran a small department and being a consulting company, it meant keeping everyone busy with billable hours. I also ran projects and worked directly with clients. All of this built new kinds of confidence in myself, thanks to my line of work in a male-dominated environment.

It didn't just end there. I began to apply this new confidence in other areas such as DIY projects at home. I designed and built a multi-level wooden table for my music system, CDs and tapes. Each shelf was precisely the right height with no wasted space. Being able to resolve technical and other challenges at work and later at home, gave me a sense of self-confidence around the use of my I-M. I would not have had this if I, as a woman, had not allowed myself to delve into my I-M during my childhood and again during this phase of my life.

Not surprisingly at that time, in the areas of my life requiring softer skills, I did not have as much confidence.

That remained so until I began to reintegrate my feminine side. Then similarly I began to develop confidence in those areas: creating healthy relationships, trusting my intuition, honoring my feelings, trusting life, managing my thoughts and emotions and learning to love and value myself.

It took time and is always a work in progress, but it illustrates why inner balance is arguably essential for different experiences of self-confidence, which contributes to self-esteem.

As I grew in wholeness, my self-confidence and self-esteem grew.

In the early Seventies studies done by Sandra Bem, Professor Emerita of Psychology at Cornell University (8) indicate that balanced people tend to have higher self-esteem and lower levels of depression and anxiety.

We tend to be our own greatest critics. Feeling inherently good about ourselves is arguably one of our greatest challenges. Cultivating balance helps us to love and appreciate ourselves as we discover who we are and what we are capable of.

4. Healthy relationships

One of the most delightful benefits is the quality of relationships that becomes available when both individuals are balanced, whole human beings.

The benefit applies to all kinds of relationships but especially intimate relationships. When both individuals are balanced it is possible to have a "relationship of two whole persons" as opposed to a "relationship of two halves."

This topic is addressed in greater detail in chapter 13 but for now, my intention is to highlight how rich and fulfilling a relationship can be when both parties are balanced.

To provide a sense of contrast, what are relationships of two halves? Simply put, they are relationships in which each individual adopts one half of the gender binary as their sense of identity. These are relationships between "opposites" who identify with stereotypical gender roles and identities.

A relationship of two whole persons is a healthy, fulfilling partnership between two balanced individuals.

It is characterized by equality, companionship, a larger framework for common or overlapping experiences, a meeting of minds, sharing, connection and fun.

> *As a student working part-time in a local pizza restaurant I noticed a couple in their forties coming in every Friday night. What stood out is how this couple engaged in the*

most delightful and animated way. I saw them coming in week after week, for months.

There was an obvious mutual respect and deep intimacy between them. Each took turns speaking and listening. The listening seemed deep and engaged, often punctuated by guffaws of laughter. It wasn't one person always laughing at the other's jokes: it was mutual.

I had to know their secret! Mustering up the courage, I walked over to them and asked, "Excuse me, but who are you and how do you manage to interact in such a delightful way?"

Their response was one of amused delight. They were a busy, married couple and Friday night was their weekly date. Both were top executives – she of a nationwide fashion store and he of a financial services firm. Although they lived together they each traveled so much and led such busy lives that they didn't have much time to connect during the week.

I later realized that each individual was whole unto him- or herself. They were coming together as two whole individuals with a lot to share about their week. They were in similar positions, and could easily relate to each other's experiences. They had much to share and had delightful ways of relating with one another. They continued to meet for their weekly chat and I continued to be amazed and amused by this couple. I will never forget the impression they made on me.

Twenty years later I found myself in a similar situation, only this time from the opposite perspective. While chatting away with my husband in a restaurant, a waitress approached us and asked the same questions: "Excuse me, but I've noticed how amazingly you interact with each other. How do you do this?" The situation had come full circle.

What are the dynamics in a relationship of two whole persons?

When both individuals are balanced each relates to other from a different "place." It is no longer the "the feminine half" and the "masculine half" relating as two separate, monolithic and opposite entities with different roles and sense of identity.

Here instead, a whole person (balanced I-F and I-M) is relating to a whole person. Each person is free to be their full, whole self. The interaction is a fluid dance between the two, with each person taking turns to lead and follow, do and be, speak and listen, and give and receive.

Being a whole person means you don't need others to "complete" you. This is because neither person has large parts of themselves that are suppressed and projected outward, requiring completion by the other.

Each person takes responsibility for their wholeness as well as their own happiness. This changes everything.

Giving is done from a desire to share, not from an obligation to be or do something expected by the other. Receiving is done with gratitude and acceptance, not from expectation.

This keeps the relationship fresh. Nothing is taken for granted.

Each person is encouraged to do what makes them happy. This does not lead to chaos. When we are balanced, whatever makes us happy could never be harmful to another. The relationship supports each person to fully be who they are and pursue their dreams.

At the same time no partner would want to burden the other with an unfair distribution for example, of domestic chores. Chores are shared as a normal, unavoidable aspect of life that each person is equally responsible for. Gender roles are blurred, if not altogether unrecognizable. Admittedly, the latter is easier for couples without children or those with adult children who have left home. However, it is still possible to have preferred roles for a time and not confuse these with one's very identity. This aspect is also explored in more detail later.

Personal and spiritual growth is different in a relationship of two whole persons. A life partner is not only a best friend, lover and companion, but someone we can learn from. Each individual has unique set of strengths and skills they bring to the relationship.

However, rather than remaining a fixed difference over a lifetime, these strengths represent enormous growth potential for the other partner. Each partner potentially serves as a role model for the other.

For example, although I have confidence in my ability to do DIY projects, my husband is more experienced and nuanced in this area. For me a nut is a nut, but for him it could be a cap nut, a square nut or a wing nut. Apart from the endless fun we have with these distinctions, doing DIY projects together is a wonderful way to connect and have fun while learning new skills.

A life partner is not only a lover and friend, but an ally in our journey to wholeness.

Given their track record, who would have thought relationships could be so good? It seems this is what the whole world is after, yet it remains elusive for so many.

The key is becoming balanced within ourselves first. This creates the conditions for attracting a similarly balanced partner. Now we have the ingredients for a healthy, loving and fulfilling relationship.

5. Work-life balance

As an executive coach, work-life balance issues come up often with my clients.

This is no wonder, given the pace of modern life. One of my clients works seven days a week and wakes up at 3 am on most days to finish his work. This may be an extreme example, yet many people's lives are heavily skewed around their work. They crave balance but they don't know how to bring it about.

We all face the challenge that comes with living in a physical world: we must somehow balance career and financial aspirations with time for ourselves, time for our spouse, time for our children, friends, family and pets, time for exercise, time for hobbies and play, and time for spiritual pursuits.

This is a tall order. How exactly do we achieve this?

The truth is: work-life balance cannot happen until we embrace and balance our I-M and I-F. Whereas I-M is the impetus to "go-go-go", to achieve, make money, climb the ladder, and become recognized for our achievements, I-F is the impetus to rest, take time out, play, have fun, get into quiet mode, connect with nature or connect with others on a personal and heartfelt level.

When these two internal complementary opposite forces are equal and balanced we have, in a sense, no choice but to live a balanced life. Slowing down or taking a break is then no longer a "nice to have" but "a luxury that I cannot afford." It becomes self-evident. Obvious. A necessity.

If work-life balance issues are a pattern, it is indicative of I-M overshadowing I-F. For some people there may be no way around it for the foreseeable future: it is a matter of survival.

For others it is not truly about survival: it is a mindset, a way of life that has crept in.

How does it happen? The world we live in with its emphasis on outer achievement is certainly conducive to this imbalance. We need to forge careers and make things work but this pressure to perform also appeals to the egoic part of us. The goal-oriented, active, driving principle in us that likes things done and to go a certain way has taken front seat. Our priorities become defined accordingly. What's missing is the balancing force of the I-F. When this is absent it is like a train with no brakes.

A concerned loved one might try to get us to stop. "Come on darling, shouldn't you take a break now?" But an outside influence doesn't hold a candle to our own ingrained habits. It can remind us but only we ourselves can make downtime a priority.

Even the knowledge "I should" is insufficient. When I-M *is* our operating system, that message gets overridden.

The only time work-life balance can happen is when your own goal-oriented, active, driving principle is balanced by your own being-oriented, rejuvenating, resting principle.

It is that simple.

Life is lived according to our priorities and those come from deep within the psyche. It is at this deep level that balance needs to be embedded. This entails our basic attitude about ourselves and life.

I heard someone say: "Your world will expand to fill every available corner until you put a boundary to it." This implies that if we take on more, life gives us more and on it goes until we draw the line in the sand - until we say "enough."

The Law of Attraction states that the external events, circumstances and people in our lives mirror that which is within us. Changing our external reality first requires an internal shift. This is why work-life balance issues reflect an internal imbalance when it comes to our I-M and I-F.

The solution is not to do "more of this activity and less of that." That is still a focus on doing. It won't last.

The only sustainable solution is to first cultivate inner balance.

Once we have cultivated this our priorities shift accordingly, different choices are made and creative solutions present themselves.

6. Effective leadership

There are two contexts for effective leadership: leading people in smaller teams and leading a business. The term I use to describe a business that is run effectively by a balanced leader is "conscious business."

Individual leadership

A major benefit of being balanced is that it creates effective leadership.

Studies show that to be truly effective as a leader you need to have as much focus on relationship-building as you have on a drive for results. In a study by Zenger and Folkman (9) 25,000 leaders were rated for leadership effectiveness by 200,000 individuals, their stakeholders.

Only 13% of the leaders who scored high in *either* relationship building *or* drive for results made it into the top 10% echelon of leaders. However, *72% of leaders who scored high in both relationship building and drive for results made it into the top echelon.*

This indicates that in order to be a top leader, it is necessary to have enlivened both aspects: "relationship building" (I-F) and "drive for results" (I-M).

These two elements, when combined in a leader are *more than 5 times more effective than each element on its own*. This is a measurable outcome of the *Law of Balance*: the power and synergy of I-M and I-F operating in a dynamic state of balance.

Inner balance is essential for leadership effectiveness. Leadership involves people. Nobody wants to be dictated to by the equivalent of a military general. A dogged focus on hard work and results communicates the message "we don't care about you or your wellbeing – we only care about the results you can bring us."

Even the most self-motivated person is eventually going to become resentful of a message that focuses on the need for results at the expense of personal wellbeing. The message we as leaders and managers send out to others is crucial. It is an accepted fact that disgruntled employees do not leave their place of work; they leave their manager.

At the same time leadership is not only about building relationships and being popular. People also need a leader with a drive for results, someone who can have the tough conversations and be assertive when needed.

That is the point: it is not one or the other. It is both.

Inner balance gives us the ability to be both. It is the key to effective leadership.

Conscious Business

A related benefit of inner balance is that it enables what is now widely known as "conscious business."

For the past several years I have taught an MBA course on this topic. It is apparent that this course is a game changer for many of the MBA students, particularly those who already run their own businesses. Students learn that business can be profitable and yet contribute to the greater good in a way that goes far beyond ordinary corporate social responsibility.

Here is a brief explanation: a conscious business operates from a higher purpose than just profit-making. It aims to create genuine value for its major stakeholders while reaping the financial rewards of its value-adding activities in a win-win situation.

Major stakeholders include shareholders, employees, customers, suppliers, the community and environment. Ordinary business is designed to maximize shareholder returns but more often than not this ends up being a win-lose situation. While profits are essential to any business, this becomes "profits at all costs."

In a conscious business the value is returned to the business via a complex set of feedback loops. Rather than each stakeholder fighting for a bigger piece of the same pie, the focus is on creating a larger pie. Everyone gets a share of the positive outcome.

According to John Mackey and Raj Sisodia, co-authors of Conscious Capitalism (10), examples of such businesses include Google, Wegmans, REI, Whole Foods, The Container Store, Southwest Airlines and Starbucks, to name a few. This is not to say these businesses are perfect but they do operate successfully based on conscious business principles and more successfully than their ordinary business counterparts.

Mackey and Sisodia have stated that in order to run a business consciously its leaders must possess a balance of I-M and I-F qualities.

> *Leaders need to be fully integrated human beings who transcend typical dualities; they are strong and loving, masculine and feminine, and have high standards of excellence and a high degree of emotional intelligence.*

They go on to confirm a growing social trend that is central to the message of this book: Most of us, men and women alike, are becoming better at integrating the masculine and feminine sides of our personae.

The authors acknowledge that a balance of I-M and I-F is crucial to running a conscious business.

The focus, analytical thinking and drive of the I-M needs to function in alignment with the compassionate, big picture view of the I-F. One without the other simply will not create the desired results.

The outcome is the ability to co-create a successful, profitable business and a better world at the same time. As an added impetus, Mackey and Sisodia have shown that these businesses financially outperform ordinary businesses in the short and long term.

7. Purpose-driven life

Another outcome of inner balance is the ability to create a purpose-driven life.

The topic of "life purpose" can be stressful especially when we are feeling unsure about our purpose. What if our purpose is what we choose it to be? For some, a sense of life purpose may feel inborn and for others it may be something they are focusing on and creating right now. I believe we can have more than one purpose at any time and our purpose/s may change over time. This is because we have free will and life is our opportunity to explore and grow through experience.

To live a purpose-driven life may include anything from giving expression to an inborn sense of purpose to simply doing what you love and going where you feel guided to be.

In an interview with Professor Emeritus and Near-Death Experience (NDE) researcher Kenneth Ring (11), a woman named Peggy spoke of revelations she received during her NDE:

> *One thing I [learned] was that we are ALL here to do an "assignment of love." We don't have to do it at all, or we can do as many as we like. It's up to us. Our "assignment" is programmed in at birth and it is the very thing or things we love most. I was such a bozo. I always thought doing what you loved most was selfish. I can remember how amazed and happy I was when this information "came into my mind." This other source of energy [a being of light] using my voice said, "That is the most unselfish and constructive thing you can do for the world because that is your assigned energy and you will be happiest doing it, best at it, and most respected for it!"*

Peggy's account confirms that our purpose is to do the very things we love most.

As palliative care nurse Bronnie Ware's research points out (7) as mentioned before, few people actually experience the joy of living their lives on purpose.

So where does balance come into this?

In simple terms, your I-F serves as your compass, that part of you that can intuit, feel and receive guidance on your sense of purpose and next steps. Your I-M is the ability to take action.

As long as you are internally balanced, you will be able take action in alignment with your inner compass. This leads to being in the flow of your life and opens the way to synchronicities.

Your compass, which operates by way of your feelings and intuition, guides you to make the most inspired choices for yourself. Your I-F capability for self-awareness enables you to recognize where your talents and interests lie. You might have a wide range of interests but your I-F tells you where to focus your attention at this time.

Without the I-F, we have limited direction. We might lead a busy life full of activity and we might even have gained worldly success. This is not the same as a fulfilling or purposeful life. Without the I-F, life is a series of events, meetings and deadlines – being busy with the hope that it leads to fulfilment. Without inner guidance we are doomed to a life involving lots of trial and error - surely the least efficient way to happiness and living a purposeful life. It is far more efficient to tap in to our feelings and let our intuition guide us.

Without the I-M we would not have the necessary drive or confidence to take action and make our dreams a reality. Even if we have inspiring ideas and dreams – or may be nudged into the perfect career or relationship - we would not take the action. Opportunities would be missed.

Before visiting the university campus to check out the possibility of studying the MA in Consciousness Studies I was unsure whether this would be part of my next steps or not. After all it was expensive. I would be in a country without the right to work except part-time on campus. If I had followed simple logic and "done the math" I would have turned away from the idea of moving to the US and viewed the pursuit of this particular degree as folly.

Yet, as I stepped onto the university campus in June 1998 I had a "bliss attack." My entire body shivered with goose bumps. I knew in that instant that I would study there and that this was where I needed to be.

As mentioned before, this was one of the best decisions I have ever made and the greatest gift I have ever given myself.

It transformed my life in the direction it needed to go and this book is one of the outcomes of that experience.

In retrospect, following my inner guidance and pursuing the graduate degree in California against all the odds was an important step on my path and for me it was part of my experience of living a purpose-drive life. On the other hand, writing this book feels like the expression of a desire I have had since I was a little child – to examine who we really are and what role gender really serves, and provide a fresh new perspective that is positive, liberating and healing.

Living a purpose-filled life means habitually being open to receiving inner guidance so that we can heed its call and take action that aligns with it.

This could result in small actions like telephoning a particular person who ends up having just the information we needed, or it could result in large actions, like moving to a different location, starting a family, writing a book or starting your own business.

8. Moving beyond patriarchy

It was during my spiritual quest when I began to look beneath surface appearances that it occurred to me that patriarchy is not in itself a cause, but rather a symptom of something deeper.

I realized that patriarchy is a mindset in which I-M and its physical expressions are considered better than or more valuable than I-F and its expressions.

This is a mindset and it has very real effects to be explored in chapter 7.

If you are in a female body your greatest contribution to moving past patriarchy is cultivating inner balance.

As women we also need to heal our pain around it and move past seeing ourselves as victims.

Being balanced enables us to stand up for ourselves where boundaries have been crossed, to draw a line in the sand and say "no more." In essence we draw from our I-M to set new boundaries and stand up for ourselves.

This is an essential part of breaking the perpetrator-victim cycle that characterizes a patriarchal society.

If you are in a male body, your greatest contribution toward moving past patriarchy is cultivating inner balance. This will help you find healthier expressions of masculinity.

Being balanced enables men to refrain from overstepping other people's boundaries or resorting to "male privilege" even in subtle ways. For example, rather than letting a female partner take more than half of the responsibility for domestic chores, men can literally step up to the dirty plate and take equal responsibility.

Inner balance enables men and women to co-create an external reality that reflects the inner reality: the equal valuation, love for I-F and I-M.

Patriarchy hurts everything including humans, animals and the planet because unbalanced I-M tends to see people and things for their utilitarian value regardless of their wellbeing. This is how factory farming came into being and how the unmitigated race to technology has also created the conditions for climate change.

Unbalanced men also suffer by adopting this mindset. By virtue of closing themselves off from their I-F, they are effectively cutting themselves off from their humanity, their soul, their connection to the Divine. It also cuts off the possibility of having harmonious relationships. Given that women are often quite expressive of their feelings in a relationship, this can be a high price to pay.

It is sobering to know that patriarchy is something we all participate in on a subtle level - until we become conscious and begin to shift.

We tend to gravitate toward our I-M in many ways: having a preference for doing over being; working and achieving over resting and recouping; taking a short term over a long term view; relying on what we can see, touch, feel and measure over things that are subtle in nature; using logic rather than trusting our intuition and looking to the outside world for solutions to our problems rather than being introspective and delving into our feelings.

All of these examples represent a preference for I-M over I-F.

The Law of Balance

The solution to patriarchy rests with each and every one of us. The way to end the imbalance is to see it for what it is and cultivate its antidote: inner balance.

Patriarchy will only stop when sufficient numbers of people embody their I-M and I-F as *part of themselves.* The reason is quite simple: a healthy person cannot knowingly hurt "that which is me" or "like me." We more easily turn a blind eye to the hurt being caused to someone who is deemed "not like me" – for example, someone of the opposite sex.

A sustainable solution to the imbalance of patriarchy is creating inner balance. This would be nothing less than the revolution of our times - a revolution from within.

9. A step on your journey to Self-realization

Cultivating a state of balance and harmony between the I-M and I-F is a significant step forward on your path to Self-realization. Why? Because balance and harmony *is* the essence of Source. Self-realization is recognizing oneself as an embodiment of Source.

As one Near-Death Experiencer (NDEr), Sandra Rogers (12) put it when she encountered what she termed the Light:

> *God is in all of us. God is male and female, all races, and the reason for all religions.*

Peggy, the NDEr previously mentioned (11) in this chapter, said:

> *I clearly and instantly knew the light was not just a Light but was ALIVE! It had a personality and was intelligence beyond comprehension.... I knew the light was a being. I also knew that the light being was God and was genderless.*

If we want to reconnect with our true nature as Source we must go beyond our sense of being either male or female, and open up to our wholeness.

Many spiritual leaders and gurus provide meditations, mantras and philosophies designed to help us along our path to Self-realization.

These are powerful and essential aids on the path to enlightenment. However, very few mention - let alone emphasize - one of the most basic and essential keys to enlightenment: cultivating inner balance.

Where is that message? It should be sung from the rooftops.

As we will see in chapter 5 this message was in fact spoken by Jeshua (the Aramaic name for Jesus) but it was not generally understood and was disregarded along with other esoteric teachings that did not fit into the status quo.

If we want to embrace and embody our true nature as God consciousness we must cultivate the same harmonious integration of I-M and I-F energies that Source represents.

Cultivating your own inner balance is a massive step in your journey to enlightenment.

10. Co-creating a better world

No matter what we are creating – cell phones, cars, business solutions, legal transactions, food, clothing, schools or communities - balance and wholeness enables us to create outcomes that are both functional *and* beneficial; technically accurate *and* conducive to health; efficient *and* humanitarian; effective *and* environmentally safe.

Whether you are a CEO, a nurse, a teacher, a coach, a parent or a software engineer; whatever you bring forth into the world will be the most effective, most loving, most thoughtful version of itself if it comes from a place of balance.

Why is this outcome automatic? With our I-F in place we care for people, animals and the environment. We can see the big picture. We are good at communication, collaborating and negotiating. Our heart is open. We are guided by our conscience.

With our I-M in place we automatically have a bias for action, work and the achievement of our objectives. We are willing to take risks.

When these two sides operate harmoniously, what we do can only make the world a better place.

A few years ago my husband and I were house hunting. After seeing the available options, we decided to focus on one particular area designed by Garden Cities - in my own words, "a conscious town planning company." Garden Cities is a non-profit organization with a wholly balanced mindset and the finest expertise. They have been designing highly integrated, human-friendly suburbs and homes since 1919. By "integrated" I mean each area is designed to have the right number of shops, schools, a hospital, community sports grounds, sidewalks, bicycle lanes, parks and green belts where people can live and exercise in a beautiful and safe setting. The suburb is designed holistically with utter precision borne of years of experience. Being a non-profit organization, the levies for maintenance are not high.

This is what balance creates and looks like. It stands head and shoulders above anything that is less balanced.

One of the benefits of balancing your I-M and I-F is that you will automatically be co-creating a better world – just by being who you are and pursuing your particular set of interests and talents.

What happens in an unbalanced society that adheres to the gender binary?

One half loses sight of their I-F, their humanity, their conscience and can only seem to find an interest in more power, more money, moving further up the hierarchy, and "winning" at the game of life, which is seen as a giant competition. All of this is strived for no matter the cost to others or the planet.

The other half loses sight of their own I-M, their *chutzpah*, assertiveness, rightful personal power and natural authority in a world that actually needs their direction and needs them to take a firm stand.

In a balanced society everything comes together beautifully.

To create a better world, we need to advance a message of balance to younger generations.

Let us stop raising our children according to the gender binary and what it means to be "a real man" or "a real woman." Let us raise the next generations to embrace their wholeness while pursuing their own unique interests and aspirations. Let us instill this "freedom to be" in ourselves, and in the next generation from a young age.

Starting with ourselves, this will be our greatest hope and contribution toward a sustainable future and a better world.

CHAPTER 5

Is Inner Balance a New Idea?

Is the idea of inner balance a new age theory or does it come from antiquity?
The call for inner balance is not new at all.
Such calls have come from far and wide throughout the ages. The earliest inscriptions of yin and yang were found on bones at around 1400 BCE (Before the Common Era) (13) and *Awen*, the Celtic symbol for masculine-feminine balance was written about by Nennius in 796 AD based on earlier works by the Welsh monk Gildas (14).
This chapter highlights different spiritual paths and individuals who have specifically called upon us to balance our I-M and I-F energies.
For much of our human history, however, only a small minority have been able to understand and apply the wisdom. I'll explore some reasons why this may be so in the next two chapters. However, as a society this is something we have been struggling with. After all, the gender binary - the idea that we can be either masculine or feminine but not both - is still prevalent in today's world.

Great minds have called for balance

The purpose of this chapter is not an in-depth exploration of the spiritual paths or individuals who have called for balance, but to highlight who has called for it and the language they use to do so.
Here you will come across some well-known advocates for balance. There may also be some surprises.

Taoism

This ancient Chinese philosophy calls us to bring our yin (I-F) and yang (I-M) into a state of dynamic balance. Doing so brings us into alignment with the Tao, The Way of the universe and nature. This in turn opens us to receive support and abundance from the universe in the form of health, happiness and prosperity.

For me, this articulates and represents the *Law of Balance*.

The Tao, or Oneness, gave birth to the universe of the ten thousand things (the great diversity of things). Lao Tzu, author of the *Tao Te Ching*, stated:

> *The ten thousand things carry yin and yang. They achieve harmony by combining these forces.*

Yin is the negative, receptive, feminine principle in nature. Yang is the positive, active, masculine principle. The term "negative" should not be confused with "negativity" or "evil" but is akin to the negative pole of a magnet. It is purely a matter of charge, but is no indication of virtue or the lack thereof.

In fact, in Taoism the feminine principle is highly valued. Lao Tzu wrote:

> *Know the masculine, but keep to the feminine.*

He also emphasized that "the weak" will overcome "the strong" just like running water eventually eats its way into cement. Here "weak" refers to our ability to be soft and yielding when going about our affairs, rather than willful and forceful. There is a time and place for everything, but generally, he says, we should stay closely in touch with our yin.

Everything has yin and yang in it. The yin and yang forces are never really separated; Yin contains the seed of yang within it and vice versa. Therefore, nothing can remain in its yin state or its yang state for very long. Life is a flow between yin and yang, and inner balance enables us to live in the flow.

Gnostic gospels

Jeshua was not only a proponent of inner balance, he lived it.

Two of the most beautiful sources of channeled information I've come across about the life of Jeshua are *Anna, grandmother of Jesus* by Claire Heartsong (2002) and *The Jeshua Channelings* by Pamela Kribbe (2008). These books speak of a fundamental belief in the inner balance of I-M and I-F as an essential part of Essene mysticism. This was the philosophy and spiritual path Jeshua was raised in.

A disciple asks Jeshua: "How do we get into the kingdom of heaven?" In today's language this might be phrased as: "How do we attain enlightenment or Self-realization?"

His answer is identically captured in two Gnostic gospels – the Gospel of the Beloved Companion (30:12) and the Gospel of Thomas (22):

> *When you make the two into one, and when you make the inner like the outer and the outer like the inner, and the upper like the lower, and when you make male and female into a single one, so that the male will not be male nor the female be female.... only then shall you gain the kingdom.*

Jeshua is speaking of rising above the duality of male and female, and integrating them so that a man is not only I-M and a woman is not only I-F. *Then* we will be able to become Self-realized (enter the kingdom) because only then are we truly in alignment with Source.

For me, writing this book took courage but it must have taken enormous courage to say this two thousand years ago when very few would have had the ears to hear. As can be expected, most of the disciples were confused by his answer and were reported to be grumbling among themselves, except for Mary Magdalene and Thomas who seemed to understand.

In keeping with the church's lust for power and privilege in a patriarchal era, the idea of balancing the I-M and I-F was no doubt a threat, and was therefore eliminated from official church doctrine. Fortunately, texts from the Gnostic gospels have shown us differently.

It is no leap of imagination to think that Jeshua exemplified inner balance.

When we consider his teachings, he was advocating for humility, kind-heartedness, surrendering to divine guidance, coming from a place of love, yielding (turning the other cheek), empathy (do unto others) and forgiveness.

Few people may have interpreted it this way, but in essence this is a call for people to integrate their I-F. During a patriarchal era, this is the required next step to achieve inner balance and a higher state of consciousness.

Vedic Philosophy

In Vedic philosophy, Brahman (Source) is described as the seamless integration of two complementary opposites: silence and dynamism. Silence is associated with inner knowing and dynamism with action. Sound familiar? We humans are said to be at our most effective when we can balance these two complementary opposites.

In the words of Maharishi Mahesh Yogi:

> *Brahman integrates these opposite values of silence and activity. Silence is Gyanshakti (Gyan = knowledge, Shakti = power) and activity is Kriyashakti (Kriya = action, Shakti = power). This Brahman is made of these two opposite values, silence and dynamism, but at the same time it remains completely unified. On this level there is no difference between silence and dynamism. This field of the perfect union of the two opposite values defines the consciousness of the ideal ruler.*

Ideal leadership is defined as having a balance of these fundamental complementary opposites: silence and dynamism or knowledge and action.

Consistent with the message in this book, we are called upon to balance these two complementary opposite aspects that are foundational to Brahman (Source) and are unified in Brahman.

This message from Vedic Philosophy is utterly consistent with the call to balance the I-M and I-F.

The Hindu Tantra

Tantra is an ancient Hindu tradition of beliefs, meditation and ritual practices that seeks to channel the divine energy of Brahman into the human microcosm (15). The Tantric practitioner uses prana (subtle energy flowing through the universe, including one's body) to attain goals which may be spiritual, material or both (16). Tantra, rather than being based on philosophy or science, is a technique based on experience.

During a series of talks, Osho (17) states:

> *No one is just male and no one is just female; everyone is bisexual. Both sexes are there. This is a very recent research in the West, but for tantra this has been one of the most basic concepts for thousands of years. You must have seen some pictures of Shiva as Ardhanarishwar – half man, half woman. There is no other concept like it in the whole history of man. Shiva is depicted as half man, half woman.*

Osho acknowledges that adepts of Hindu Tantra have known for thousands of years what science is now beginning to tell us: that no human being is entirely male or female; we are different blends of both and that this is natural.

Native American philosophy

Native American cultures have historically acknowledged five genders including male, female, two-spirit male or female (a male or female with balanced I-M and I-F) and transgender.

In an article titled "Two Spirits, One Heart, Five Genders" published on Jan 23, 2016 in *Indian Country Today*, Duane Brayboy states:

> *The Two Spirit people in pre-contact Native America were highly revered and families that included them were considered lucky. Indians believed that a person who was able to see the world through the eyes of both genders at the same time was a gift from The Creator.*

Native American elders, Chief Standing Elk and Grandmother Silverstar, have emphasized the value of bringing the I-M and I-F aspects into a state of balance and harmony. This state of being, they argue, reflects our true nature.

Chief Standing Elk has identified 22 universal laws for spiritual development (18). Half of these represent feminine energy and the other half, masculine energy. This shows that I-F and I-M are equally represented in the cosmic order of things. For us to develop spiritually, we need to master all of these aspects.

Here is a short excerpt from his book:

> *Honor each other as Man and as Woman – without each other you cannot live, without each other you cannot grow. You are in balance as human beings. You are one as human beings. As a human being you are the same energy, only with the different name – Man, Woman.*

Chief Standing Elk acknowledges men and women as interdependent beings of different sexes, yet emphasizes that on a spiritual level we are the same energy, and this energy, like the universe, is a balance of I-M and I-F.

Martinus, a 19th century mystic

Martinus was a Danish mystic who lived around the turn of the twentieth century. His story is fascinating and his ideas enlightening. These are captured beautifully by Else Byskov in *Death is an Illusion* (19). This brief write-up cannot do justice to the man he was, but I will provide a context of who he is before getting to his ideas on inner balance.

Martinus extolled the virtues of balancing the I-M and I-F as a way for us to operate more closely in alignment with our souls. He believed that men and women were ordinarily completely dominated by either their masculine or feminine pole. He called these "one-poled beings."

The consequences of being a one-poled being are many, he argued, and include intense competitiveness with those of the same sex and an unavoidable neediness and insecurity that exists in relationships with the opposite sex.

The solution, he argued, is to develop both sides of oneself and become whole. Then, he felt, relationships are capable of true love. As an individual one is then operating in alignment with the nature of God, who exemplifies this wholeness.

Martinus believed that Jeshua was completely balanced.

> *Although Jesus appeared in the body of a man, he was not really a man. He was a human being. The human being in the image and likeness of God is neither a man or a woman. The human being in the image and likeness of God has his I-M and I-F poles in balance. That means that the female pole has reached the same level of unfolding as the male pole.*

Martinus believed that everyone is capable of balance. One of his more controversial ideas was that gays and lesbians are more highly developed than heterosexual individuals because they inherently embody a more balanced state of being.

Carl Jung

The psychiatrist Carl Jung advocated for inner balance. In order to be psychologically healthy, he felt, men must integrate their anima and women, their animus.

The animus is linked to the intellect, mind, focused consciousness and respect for facts. The anima is linked to the soul, imagination, fantasy and play. (20)

If we don't integrate these "opposite aspects" he argued, we end up projecting them onto our partner, setting up the conditions for attachment, co-dependence and conditional love.

Rather than projecting onto others and hoping that these other persons will "complete" us, he believed that we are far better off if we can integrate our opposite sex energies and become whole persons.

Akhenaten

King Amenhotep IV, who later changed his name to Akhenaten, was an Egyptian pharaoh who lived in the 14th century BCE. He ruled for 17 years and was husband to Queen Nefertiti.

Akhenaten, a controversial figure, has been speculated about more than any other character in Egyptian history. Often called the originator of monotheism and the world's first recorded individual, he has fascinated and inspired many including Sigmund Freud. Freud argued that Moses had been a priest in the same lineage as Akhenaten, and was forced to leave Egypt with his followers after Akhenaten's death.

Akhenaten was a religious revolutionary. He introduced a new religion, the worship of Aten, a monotheistic sun God to take the place of the traditional Egyptian religion of polytheism.

> *Because the god Aten was referred to as "the mother and father of all humankind" it has been suggested that Akhenaten was made to look androgynous in artwork as a symbol of the androgyny of the god (21).*

Indeed, Akhenaten had himself depicted in a variety of statues and images ranging from lean warrior-like figures to feminine portrayals of himself with curvy hips, large breasts, thick thighs and a pregnant belly. Akhenaten was observably at peace with his I-M and I-F aspects.

His egalitarian worldview extended to his relationship with Queen Nefertiti. Together they co-reigned and shared power and responsibilities in a way that was far more egalitarian than the status quo favored.

Modern champions for inner balance

Modern scientists, philosophers and business people have spoken of the need to balance the I-M and I-F. These include Deepak Chopra, Marianne Williamson, Ken Wilber, John Mackey, Diana Cooper, Amit Goswami, and Margaret Wheatley.

Famous balanced individuals

There have been examples of great individuals who are distinguishable by their balance of I-M and I-F energies.

My list would include Leonardo da Vinci, Sir Isaac Newton, Jeshua, Mary Magdalene, Hildegard von Bingen, Queen Elizabeth I, Queen Marie Therese, Mozart, Abraham Lincoln, Eleanor Roosevelt, Einstein, Marie Curie, Martin Luther King Jnr, Mother Theresa and Nelson Mandela.

In each of these towering figures the tantalizing combinations can be seen: strong and empathic; outspoken and introspective; logical and intuitive; assertive and humanitarian; precise and imaginative; bold and beneficent.

To explore just one example, Leonardo da Vinci is widely considered to be one of the most intelligent people who ever lived. He is famous for his abilities as a painter, sculptor, architect, musician, mathematician, engineer, inventor, anatomist, geologist, cartographer, botanist, and writer.

Arguably, the key to his genius is that he was exceptionally developed in both his I-M and I-F aspects. He is as famous for his accurate and insightful engineering designs as he is for his rich, colorful and nuanced art. Moreover, his engineering designs are not only functional, they also have a certain beauty to them. His paintings and sculptures are not only beautiful and subtle but the human features are accurately depicted.

CHAPTER 6

Can We Really Balance?

Is it really possible to balance?
We come into the world with a body that presents itself as male or female. One exception is intersex anatomy which occurs in 0.5% of people (22).

Biological differences between the sexes are embedded in the genetics and hormones.

So how is it possible that we could balance?

Perspectives from body, mind and spirit

If biology were a binary option between male and female and we were merely biological beings, then the answer would be: no, we cannot become balanced.

However, there is a growing argument that there is no biological binary; we are more of a mixture of male and female than originally thought. Steven Epstein, Associate Professor of Sociology at the University of California in San Diego writes (23):

> *Sex differences, like all differences in nature, lie on a continuum, and they become evident through statistical aggregation: there is no unambiguous dividing line between the two sexes, and every criterion of differentiation that might be invoked, from genitalia to hormones to chromosomes, fails to perform a strict demarcating function.*

Biological sex exists not as a binary but a continuum. Even genetics, hormones and genitalia – traditionally the indicators of biological sex – lie on a continuum. A 2011 BBC documentary "Me, my sex and I" (24) showed that it is more common than previously thought for men and women to have different permutations and combinations of five indicators of biological sex, each of which occurs on a sliding scale. These are the presence of male or female chromosomes; the presence of sperm or egg; the absence or presence of a womb; male or female sex hormones; and male or female genitalia.

A new study from Tel Aviv University seems to confirm this by discovering that human brains do not fit neatly into "male" and "female" categories (25). Instead, our brains seem to share a patchwork of forms, some more common in males, others more common in females, and some common to both.

Recognizing that these patterns represent some degree of sex differences, the research team, led by behavioral neuroscientist Daphne Joel, opted to create a continuum of brain structures ranging from "maleness" to "femaleness."

Imagine a stereotypical male brain and a stereotypical female brain on either end of the spectrum. The team discovered that up to 8% of people fell into these end categories. Only 8% of men and women have stereotypical male or female brains, respectively. The vast majority displayed permutations and combinations of both to greater or lesser degrees.

This acknowledges there are some sex differences, but it suggests that even from a *purely biological standpoint* we already display some degree of balance, or the potential for it.

That provides an indication of our ability to balance based purely on the body. We are more than a body.

We have a mind. We have cognition. We have choice.

The mind is very powerful. This is why socialization or conditioning plays a significant role in shaping us: the mind can buy into socialized ideas of who we are supposed to be, how we're supposed to act, and *voila*, we embody those values and start to become that.

Annie, a yoga teacher in her mid-forties reminisces about her childhood:

> *When I was three or four years old I used to climb jungle gyms, but I insisted on wearing long dresses and even had to have a bit of heel. I wanted to be free but I felt I had to look the part. I did a lot of the things boys did like play with matches and play out in the park, but I had to look the part.*

While Annie was open enough to let herself climb jungle gyms, she had a built-in concept of how she had to look in order to be acceptable regardless of the comfort or safety involved. This is conditioning.

Keeping an open and questioning mind is imperative for going beyond conditioning and moving into our authentic nature. Attitudes and beliefs play an enormous role in our ability to become balanced.

The evidence suggests there is greater scope for balance than was previously thought, and it probably varies from person to person depending on biology and beliefs.

Now I would like to look more closely at the role played by the soul.

The highest part of the soul, or Higher Self - what we aspire to reawaken in ourselves - is by nature, balanced. This would seem to open up the possibilities for balance even more. However, the degree to which we can access this part of ourselves depends on where we are in our spiritual journey.

The more spiritually evolved we are - the closer we are to our spiritual nature - the easier it is to balance. For a spiritually inclined person balance is very much available. The next step is really about understanding what it means to be balanced and how to get there.

From a spiritual perspective balance is available to everyone at some point on their journey, but not to everyone right now because we are all at different points on this journey. "Old souls" will find it easier, having experienced a variety of different roles and personas. "Young souls" will find it harder; having their hands full just learning to master skills typically associated with their gender.

Thus, being balanced is not for everyone right now.

However, if the question is: "can we be *more* balanced?" the answer is most likely to be "yes." Everyone can benefit from being at least *more* balanced.

Balance as part of our collective purpose

I would like to propose an alternative to the traditional creation story and our purpose within it.

Source chose to usher a portion of itself forth to embark on an adventure in self-discovery, creativity and expansion.

To provide the ideal "playground" for this endeavor, the universe of form and duality was created.

As sparks of the Divine, we were created and set free to undertake our own individual journeys of discovery. Since we are connected to Source our personal discoveries are expansive and illuminating to Source whether our behavior is deemed by us to be "good" or "bad." We have free will. There is no judgement from Source however every action has consequences – painful or rewarding.

This is karma but its purpose is not punishment. The soul desires opportunities to balance previous actions and to understand the implications of its own actions through experience. This is part of realizing who we are by discovering who we are not. It is part of the journey of realizing our true nature as Source. Our growth and creativity are expansive to us as they are to Source.

In the words of Mellen-Thomas Benedict, a Near-Death Experiencer quoted in *Lessons from the Light* by Kenneth Ring (11):

We are God getting to know God through us.

A similar idea is shared in the *Teachings of Abraham* series by Esther and Jerry Hicks (26):

That is really what we are all about. Source is, through all of you, finding higher and higher frequencies. The stakes are becoming more satisfying to all of us. The misconception is that Source has got it all figured out and that that's finished and perfect, and that humans are still vying for that understanding. But what's really going on is Source is expanding into greater capacities of love through that which you are living.

The closer we are to being an embodied expression of Source, the greater our capacity to express this love in ever higher forms. This is our collective purpose.

Since Source is a harmonious blend of masculine and feminine, inner balance is our destiny. The more we attain it, the more we can fulfil our greatest purpose.

Masculine and feminine energy as two universal poles

In order to create a set-up for this grand "project of love" I believe Source teased apart the portion of itself about to manifest – into its two constituent and complementary opposite poles: masculine and feminine energy.

These energy poles form the basis of the physical universe of form and duality. They are not visible but their manifestations are. This is much like the two poles of a magnet. The magnetic lines at the north pole are outward flowing (like masculine energy) whereas those at the south pole are inward flowing (like feminine energy). The poles are not visible but they, and the magnetic field between them, are real and have real effects that can be discerned and experienced.

Manifestations of this masculine-feminine duality include: day and night, incoming tides and outgoing tides, magnetic north and south poles, protons and electrons, particles and waves, acids and alkalis, zeros and ones, logic and intuition, and head and heart. It is infused throughout the universe.

The feminine and masculine poles underlying the physical universe are available for us to tap into *within ourselves*. These poles are personally experienced by us as our I-F and I-M.

You may notice that I did not include "male and female" in the list of manifestations of the masculine-feminine duality above. This is for a good reason and is explained in the *harbinger hypothesis*.

Introducing the Harbinger Hypothesis

A harbinger is one who brings forth. The harbinger hypothesis states that on the whole, men are the *harbingers* of I-M and women are the harbingers of I-F. When I say "on the whole" there are always exceptions. Some women are harbingers of I-M and vice versa. Consider gender non-conforming individuals.

In case the harbinger hypothesis may appear to pigeonhole men and women: it does not. This is only the beginning of the story.

Harbingers are not owners

Harbingers bring forth but they do not "own" these energies. Harbingers introduce certain energies into the world so that others can learn from them. They potentially serve as way-showers, but are not owners.

> *Every human being is the owner of both I-M and I-F energies.*

I-M is *not* the domain of men, nor I-F the domain of women. As an example, the word "emasculate" is only ever used in popular culture when defending a man's right to embrace his masculine side. But since we are all owners of I-F and I-M, it is just as possible to emasculate a woman. Laws and social norms that keep women invisible and in the background, less educated and unable to make their mark on the world are emasculating to women.

We each have the right to embrace and own both sides of ourselves.

Penelope is a 31-year old business entrepreneur with modern values. Born in the UK, she runs an herbal essences farm in Malawi. Coming from an entrepreneurial family that lived in different countries, she has adventure and entrepreneurship in her blood.

> *I like setting up businesses and running them for five years, and then selling them. I realize I like five-year projects. Business normally extends longer than that. But I like setting them up and then moving on.*

Clearly in touch with her I-M, Penelope was encouraged by her parents to develop both sides of herself while growing up. However, on the whole she leaned more to her I-M because her father was a significant role model.

> *I am very much both masculine and feminine energy but my masculine side was stronger for a very long time.*

Penelope's father – a man with an abundance of I-M – served as a role model for her to develop these energies *in herself.*

This illustrates the point: being a harbinger of masculine energies doesn't make him the "owner" of them. It does not give him any kind of exclusive right to these energies. He brings them forth – as men from his generation were conditioned to do - but the I-M that he embraced in himself is available for Penelope to embrace in herself.

This is exactly what Penelope did. By observing him, she integrated her own I-M as part of who she is. Her father may have played the role of harbinger but Penelope took possession of her own I-M.

Back to the earlier discussion about the manifestations of the universal masculine-feminine duality: men and women *are* manifestations *but only insofar as they are harbingers.* As individuals, men and women – except the most unbalanced ones - are different permutations and combinations of these poles.

The more balanced we become, the more we are combinations of these poles and the closer we are to Source.

Relationships as paths to wholeness

The harbinger hypothesis brings a whole new perspective to relationships. Rather than being about "two halves of a whole" *relationships are learning opportunities for cultivating wholeness within oneself.*

In a relationship, if a man is more assertive and a woman more emotionally intelligent (to use a gender-stereotypical example) the man has a role model from which to learn emotional intelligence. The woman has a role model from which to enhance her assertiveness.

The point is *not* that the woman should handle all situations involving emotional intelligence henceforth and the man all instances requiring assertiveness. That would pigeonhole people into gendered roles and rob each person of the fullness of who they are.

Instead, by adopting this approach each partner learns new skills, simultaneously finding more common ground for relating with one another.

The following story illustrates the value of relationships as paths to wholeness. Penelope describes her parents, who were unable to learn sufficiently from each other to move beyond a relationship of two halves.

> *My mother is very spiritual. She has amazing intuition.*
>
> *She never rushes things. My Dad says "We need to be doing things." But she simply says "I'm happy here." So sometimes she seems to stand still but she's happy where she is. But she also has fear to do new things. Dad doesn't understand it.*

Penelope's mother is comfortable in the "being" space but this is like a foreign language to her father. He understands "doing" and taking risks.

> *My mother doesn't get stressed. Even with us [sisters] she let us go out. She tells her daughters that they are strong and equal to men.*
>
> *Her most negative emotion is she gets angry and she won't forgive easily.*
>
> *She and Dad are constantly at loggerheads. She goes on about "men." He finds that too strong. But I think it's really about the yin and yang.*

Penelope's parents typify a relationship between a man and woman who adhere to the gender binary. There is little overlap between them; they are essentially two halves. Each takes an opposing stance.

I propose that in balanced relationships each person can learn from the other and thus grow into wholeness. Penelope expresses it this way:

You're meeting them with the purpose of becoming whole yourself. I agree with that. I think my parents met to show each other things and I think actually all relationships do that.

I don't feel like I need a man to be whole [in the sense of two halves making a whole]. I feel that I need to be whole and a man is my best friend to share it with, but they're on their own journey [to wholeness].

Penelope reiterates the view that each person is on a journey to wholeness. Rather than being there to "complete us" our partner potentially helps us to become balanced and whole within ourselves.

The harbinger hypothesis identifies the "initial" role that men and women play by bringing forth I-M and I-F energies respectively into the world. Whereas conventional wisdom leaves it there as "the way things are" unconventional wisdom says this is only the beginning.

As we evolve spiritually we become more balanced

In the earlier stages of our development it is sufficient to focus on developing the qualities associated with our own sex, such as assertiveness for men and nurturing for women.

After sufficient time and experience there comes a point in our evolution when it's just not enough to develop *only* the qualities associated with our sex. By this time, we're done being wedded to one side of ourselves with the same predictable outcomes.

This is a major milestone in our spiritual development. This is when it becomes much easier to balance: we are no longer so heavily identified with our biological sex and its perceived capabilities and roles.

This opens us up to experiencing both sides of ourselves while in the physical body. The more evolved we become, the less we identify with the body as our source of identity. The more we identify with our spiritual nature the easier it is to be balanced.

How evolution has brought us to an era of balance

To put things into greater perspective it is helpful to consider our collective evolution and our next steps within it. It seems that we are being drawn into an era that is characterized by bringing things into balance. Given the excesses of the previous era (or two) this appears to be our natural next step.

Why did we have a matriarchal era and a patriarchal era?

Collectively we have done a lot of polarized exploration. The last two eras took turns at exploring the feminine (matriarchy) and the masculine (patriarchy) separately, warts and all.

Why did we have eras such as matriarchy and patriarchy? There was a genuine purpose to exploring each complementary opposite separately and by actually conforming to gender stereotypical versions of being a male or female for many thousands of years.

By identifying with one or the other aspect (but not both) we learned a lot about each in turn: its strengths and limitations. We learned what each energy brings forth on its own. Because any one energy is by itself unbalanced, we often learn through excess.

This is where our greatest strengths can become our greatest weaknesses.

Here is a story to illustrate.

> *Jane is a coaching client with whom I developed a friendship. I learned that she grew up with the message that girls are expected to be nice at all times and accommodating of others. Showing anger was considered "unfeminine." Indeed, Jane learned how to connect with people from a young age. She remembers as a young child creeping into her father's lap and seeing his delight despite the fact that he seldom showed emotions. Not surprisingly, Jane became a kind, loving and generous person. She later married and had three children. She*

used her social skills to become a real estate agent and regularly won awards as top seller.

Jane clearly had a talent for connecting with people.

The downside is that she learned to habitually put others first. While that exemplified what it meant to be a good girl or woman, it came back to bite her many times in her life. She struggled to put her needs first even when she was depleted. This risked meaning "not being nice."

As a working mother of three, Jane struggled to assert her need for help with household chores. Her husband, an alcoholic, was unable to be fully present and without his support her sons also began to renege on their chores.

"In order to keep the peace," she said, "I decided to do it myself." It didn't come without a cost: she feels burdened and angered by the load she took onto herself for many years.

In 2007, Jane and her husband made a fresh start by moving to the ocean with the idea of retiring. Within a few years she became a pillar of the community. She volunteered for a local environmental group and a local political group as well as running the townhouse complex in which they lived.

It seemed like déjà vu: everything ended up on her shoulders.

Later, due to financial need, she returned to being a real estate agent. Within two years she became a top seller – at the age of 74. It took her nearly two years to withdraw as the chairperson of the board of trustees, but she finally put her foot down and insisted that others take a turn at running the complex. Jane has scaled down her

> *other activities too and hired an assistant to help with her real estate work. She is finally becoming comfortable with prioritizing her own needs, delegating and getting help from others. This enables her to lead a sustainable lifestyle where she can shine her light in the world and at the same time be kind to herself.*

As Jane's story illustrates, the gender binary creates the container for growth and the development of certain skills. This comes at a price as we experience the extremes of a one-sided approach.

I believe that in the new era suffering is no longer a necessary ingredient for growth because the gender binary no longer needs to be the social operating system. In the new era, awareness and choice play a far larger role in our growth and development. Personal growth can happen far more quickly.

While this has been a longstanding theme in Jane's life, in the past year she has made great strides in this area by becoming more assertive and learning to make her own needs a priority. Now she can combine her great people skills with an ability to take care of herself.

Is patriarchy coming to an end?

The short answer is "yes" and the reason is simple: the universe does not tolerate imbalance for long. It has a built-in mechanism that seeks balance.

Taoism captures this beautifully with the yin-yang symbol: Yin contains a seed of yang within it, and vice versa. Wherever the pendulum has swung to one of its extremes it cannot stay there for long because the seed of the complementary opposite begins to sprout within it and the pendulum begins to swing in the opposite direction.

We see this every few seconds with the ebb and flow of the ocean, every day in the passing of day and night, every month in the changing faces of the moon and its effect on the tides, every quarter with the changing of the seasons, every year with its endings and beginnings, and in every lifetime with the cycles that bring us from birth through various phases of life to the end of our lives on the physical plane. We also see this every few thousand years with the changing of eras.

So, yes, patriarchy is ending.

Enter: the post-polarization era

The new era represents a shift along a spiral of development with the benefits gained from the previous two eras. We are now entering a time in which both I-M and I-F are necessary for us to thrive. Since we are emerging from a patriarchal era, the next step is about integrating the feminine.

As mentioned, this is not so that the feminine can become the new dominating influence, but that it can be brought alongside the masculine in partnership.

According to Alec Ross, one of America's leading experts in innovation and author of *The Industries of the future* (27), 65% of primary school age children today will enter jobs in the future that we do not yet have titles for.

What is key for future generations, he argues, is interdisciplinary studies. Those wishing to study science, technology, engineering or math must also study in the humanities. This "bridging between two worlds" is the future of technology and this is just one example of "the I-M and I-F working in partnership" previously mentioned.

I recently attended a coaching seminar about team coaching in organizations. The message was similar: "To run successful organizations, CEOs must focus not on the individual parts of the organization but on the interconnections between the parts." The speaker was highlighting the need for relationships to be built between divisions, as well as between division heads. It is not enough for each division to be functional yet have a silo mentality (operating separately).

There is a need for each employee to see the big picture and to work in an interdisciplinary way. This spells a necessary shift toward integrating I-F (relationships, connection, collaboration, mutuality, big picture) for today's CEOs wanting to run a company effectively.

Both examples show that the new era is a call to integrate our I-F and I-M so that we can navigate both worlds effectively.

In the new era learning and growth are consciously sought and willingly undertaken. This conscious and proactive approach to learning makes it more fun and effective.

We no longer need to be stuck in the same habit for 20 years. If we want to, we can consciously decide to grow in a particular way and be done in a few months or weeks. All it takes is a pro-active approach to integrating our I-M and I-F.

In this chapter we explored the question "can we balance?" While the answer is somewhat nuanced, overall it is yes, many people can, enough to cause a tipping point to usher in the new era more quickly.

CHAPTER 7

Aren't We as a Society Balanced Enough?

"Aren't we balanced enough?"

"Isn't patriarchy over?"

"Aren't women already empowered to do whatever they want these days?"

These questions come up. They may not necessarily be *your* questions, but you probably know someone who questions the need for balance. "What's the problem?" they seem to be saying.

To address this, it is best to gain your own sense of where we are. One way is to examine the evidence, which we will do in this chapter.

The doubters have a point: we *have* evolved over the past few decades. But how far have we come?

To examine the promised evidence, this chapter begins with the signs of global imbalance. How balanced are we as a society when it comes to the I-M and I-F?

This may be a rather challenging chapter to read. On the plus side, you stand to gain new insights into the question: "Aren't we already balanced enough?"

You will also gain an appreciation for the enormous contribution you will make toward personal, interpersonal and global peace by balancing your own I-M and I-F.

Before we dive in, let's take a brief look at what is meant by "patriarchy."

A new understanding of patriarchy

I define patriarchy as a preference for I-M over I-F; a bias for the masculine end of the spectrum.

For much of my life I thought it was "greedy, uncaring men taking advantage of women." But my view changed.

It occurred to me: If I were to habitually follow my head rather than my heart is this any different *in essence* to society's systemic favoring of the masculine?

For me the answer is "no."

The following seemingly different issues are *in essence* the same:

- Habitually overriding intuition and deferring to linear, logical decision-making
- Habitually overriding the need to rest while pressing on with work regardless
- Sitting back while the woman comes home after work and attends to the bulk of domestic chores and the children
- Paying women less for the same work

Each instance ultimately represents a *denial of the feminine within*.

The scale and intensity of the outcomes may differ, but the starting point is the same.

In the first two examples, which everyone probably experiences from time to time, the bias toward I-M and the *denial of our own I-F* is obvious and direct: choosing linear thinking, logic and activity over intuition and the need for rest. This hurts us, our families and loved ones.

In the next two examples, the denial of the I-F results in *the denial of women, the harbingers of the feminine*. The denial of women is a reflection of the denial of the I-F.

How does this equate? We cannot truly love, empathize with, validate or support that which we deem to be "other."

The outcome is women are systemically oppressed around the world. It hurts men too, but in different ways.

This view of patriarchy makes it widely available; something we all potentially participate in regardless of gender.

In all four examples the remedy is *getting back in touch with the I-F*, to rediscover her, cherish her and protect her *as a sacred aspect of ourselves.*

This will require unlearning. After all, patriarchy is the paradigm we were raised in. We are all shaped by it to some extent.

Due to the very nature of paradigms, they function largely below the level of awareness. They form an invisible and unconscious lens through which we view the world from a particular perspective. Without awareness we inadvertently contribute to its ongoing existence.

The external face of this paradigm is that the dominant group in society is white heterosexual males. Without awareness, everybody else is considered "other."

In a moving TED talk, Jackson Katz (28) highlights how the dominant group can be abusive and yet somehow remain invisible. He raises the issue of sexual violence against women, which is often described as "a woman's issue." As soon as men hear "woman's issue" he says, "they tune out." He takes exception to this.

Katz points out when many people hear "gender" they assume "women."

> *As if men don't have a gender. This is one of the ways that dominant systems maintain and reproduce themselves, which is to say that the dominant group is rarely challenged to even think about its dominance because that's one of the key characteristics of power and privilege – the ability to go unexamined, lacking introspection, in fact being rendered invisible in large measure in the discourse about issues that are primarily about us.*
>
> *And it is amazing how this works in domestic and sexual violence, how men have been largely erased from so much of the conversation about a subject that is essentially about men.*

Katz illustrates this in this sequence of four simple sentences. Notice how in each sentence the role of the man diminishes until it is invisible:

John beat Mary.

This is the most accurate version. It places John as the subject of the sentence. Notice what happens next:

Mary was beaten by John.

Mary was beaten.

Mary is a battered woman.

Once we get to "Mary is a battered woman" John has all but disappeared from the sentence even though he is the very reason she is battered. Now it's a "woman's issue." Pretty soon the victim blaming starts: "But what was she wearing?" and "Why doesn't she leave?"

Typically, these questions are asked rather than "Why can't John manage his emotions better?" or "What is the matter with John?"

As mentioned, it takes great courage and awareness to step back and scrutinize the prevailing paradigm and see it for what it is. It is also very liberating to do so.

Global signs of imbalance in a patriarchal era

One way to assess how society views the feminine is examining its treatment of women. Another is how it treats gay men and trans women. Here are 17 examples that affect millions, in some cases billions.

1. Distribution of household chores

This is an issue that nearly split my own family apart while I was growing up during the Seventies and Eighties. It caused enormous anguish, yet it was perpetuated because of assumptions about whose job it was and because it was convenient to assume this.

Despite the fact that women make up nearly half of the workforce in many countries (29), women still bear the brunt of child-rearing and domestic chores (30).

In *The Second Shift (2012)* (31), sociologist and University of California, Berkeley, Professor Arlie Hochschild found that in dual-career households, women still shoulder the brunt of work in the home, much like they did 20 years ago. When adding together the time spent in paid work, child care, and housework, she argues, working mothers put in a *month of work a year more* than their spouses.

This gender bias is corroborated in the US Bureau of Labor Statistics which shows that in 2014 on an average day, 20 percent of men did housework - such as cleaning or laundry - compared with 49 percent of women (32). The good news is the gap is narrowing but it may be too slow for many women.

Most people do not relish the idea of doing housework, yet it's one of those things, like brushing teeth, that has to be done and everyone should be responsible.

What does it tell us that this collective burden is still being placed onto women's shoulders, even when women work full-time outside the home? Does it demonstrate an equal appreciation for the needs of women or does it place men's needs for convenience, rest and play *above* those of women?

2. Gender pay gap

In 2014 women earned 79 cents to every dollar that a man earned in the US (33). Although this has improved from 1974 (59%) to 2014 (79%), at this pace it would take 100 years to achieve parity.

In most other countries in the world the numbers are similar or less. One study showed that in Britain, where women fare better at a nearly 87% gender pay gap, it still amounts to this: in 2015 women effectively worked for free from 9 November until the end of the year (34).

What are the effects of the gender pay gap? It is well-known that women spend the vast majority of their income on their families, thus potentially lifting entire communities out of poverty. Paying women less keeps entire communities in cycles of poverty.

The American Association for University Women (AAUW) (33) states:

> *For the 40 percent of mothers with children under the age of 18 who are their families' sole or primary breadwinner, the gender pay gap can contribute to poor living conditions, poor nutrition, and fewer opportunities for their children.*
>
> *In the US, providing equal pay to women would reduce poverty by 50% for families with a working woman. (35).*

What does the gender pay gap say about how society values women and I-F?

3. Traditionally female work is paid less

While the gender pay gap exists in nearly every field, work traditionally associated with men is better paid than work traditionally associated with women even at the same level of skill required.

There are gender differences in the choice of jobs although in 2014 approximately 60% of men and women chose fields that are not clearly traditionally male or female lines of work. Roughly 40% did.

In software development and project management jobs, where 85% of all workers are male, the average salary is between $64,000 and $68,000 per annum. By comparison, in elementary school teaching and registered nursing, where 85% of all workers are female, the average salary is between $42,000 and $55,000. Yet, all four jobs require an undergraduate degree (36).

It is a curious thing. As a society why do we value work that contributes to the built environment and technology over work that contributes to the development of a healthy society? Aren't they complementary forms of value that are mutually beneficial? Why is "more and better stuff" more important than "a healthy, functional society"?

This bias reflects the underlying imbalance: society values the masculine over the feminine.

4. Glass ceiling

What is the glass ceiling? Ann Morrison of the Center for Creative Leadership (37) describes it as a barrier "so subtle that it is transparent, yet so strong that it prevents women from moving up the corporate hierarchy."

Soraya Chemaly (38), director of the Women's Media Centre Speech Project writes (Feb 2016):

> *In the United States, white men make up more than 80% of Congress, 78% of state political executives, 75% of state legislators, 84% of mayors of the top 100 cities, 85% of corporate executive officers, 100% of CEOs of Wall Street firms, 95% of Fortune 500 CEOs, 73% of tenured professors, 64% of newsroom staffers, 97% of heads of venture capital firms, 90% of tech jobs in Silicon Valley, 97% of owners of television and radio licenses, 87% of police departments and 68% of U.S. Circuit Court Judges. Men have been 100% of our Presidents.*

Maggie Wilderotter, who in 2015 stepped down as CEO of Fortune 500 company Frontier Communications after nearly ten years at the helm, believes that the number of female chief executives is far too low, given the motivation and credentials that women hold (39).

What keeps women back?

One often cited reason for the glass ceiling is "the old-boy network" which operates behind the scenes and makes promotion decisions by selecting people who are "most like themselves" including former colleagues and old school ties. This tends to exclude women.

Yet the same bias appears to occur in "young-boy networks": A 2016 study was conducted of over 1,700 biology undergraduates at the University of Washington to identify classmates who were deemed to be "strong in their understanding of classroom material." The results were telling: The male students underestimated their female peers, and *over-nominated other men over better-performing women* (40). Male nominators showed 19 times higher gender bias, giving men a boost equivalent to an additional 0.77 GPA. Women showed very little to no bias, giving women a tiny boost of 0.04 GPA.

The strong bias against recognizing women for their high performance reflects the cultural belief that women do not excel in science and math, despite the fact that women's grades and classroom participation do not support this assumption.

Perhaps it is no different in the world of business, where women are underestimated due to deeply held cultural assumptions about their competence. This creates a glass ceiling.

Another commonly cited reason for the glass ceiling is the availability of women for top jobs. This is perhaps no wonder given that women are still shouldering the bulk of responsibility when it comes to child-raising and managing the home. As Cheryl Sandberg points out in *Lean In* (41), the role played by men in terms of being supportive, equal players on the domestic front is vital to women's success. It seems the world is waiting for men to *lean in at home.*

Despite being underrepresented in top jobs, when women make it to the top they add tremendous value to corporations. Prof. Judy Zaichkowsky of Simon Fraser University discovered that adding even one woman to a board of directors sees a positive impact on performance (42).

Moreover, companies with a high representation of women board members significantly outperform those with no female directors, according to a 2011 Catalyst analysis of financial results at Fortune 500 companies.

A 2007 McKinsey study of more than 58,000 employees in 101 organizations worldwide found significant differences in economic performance between those with at least 30 percent women in senior leadership versus those with no female representation. (43)

One reason why women may add notable value to company performance and governance is they are more willing to challenge the status quo and highlight core issues by asking the right questions. (44) Other possible reasons cited in an article by Harvard Business School Professor Emeritus, James Heskett (45) are:

> "Women have greater analytical skills and coordinate activities with much greater ease than men, while upholding company values and strategy"
>
> "Winning in this age requires more cross-disciplinary thinking... Women in my experience are better thought integrators."
>
> "Emotional intelligence could be a factor... Women tend to have more of it than men, through nurturing, but it seems that men can learn it."

Women clearly bring essential and complementary skills to the table. Yet, despite the proven benefits of having women in top positions, the norm across business is: the further up the ladder, the fewer women. Yet women's voices and wisdom, and feminine energy – whether from women or men - is arguably sorely needed in business as in every echelon of public life at the highest levels of decision-making.

What does the glass ceiling tell us about how women are valued? Why is their value doubted when the mounting evidence shows otherwise?

While some question the sanity of anyone wanting to be the CEO of a company for the hard work and long hours it requires, my response is: perhaps, but the choice should still be theirs. Chances are that if enough women become CEOs the nature of being a CEO could change and become more sustainable. One company – Whole Foods – has been known to have co-CEOs and it is a real success story.

5. Violence against women

At the United Nations Fourth World Conference on Women in Beijing in 1995, Hillary Clinton, then first lady, famously declared in front of delegates from 180 countries:

> *If there is one message that echoes forth from this conference, let it be that human rights are women's rights and women's rights are human rights, once and for all.*

Yet, the United Nations reports that violence against women is still a worldwide issue (46):

> *Violence against women and girls is not confined to any particular political or economic system, but it is prevalent in every society in the world. It cuts across boundaries of wealth, race and culture. It is an expression of historically and culturally specific values and standards which are today still executed through many social and political institutions that foster women's subservience and discrimination against women and girls.*

My heart sinks at the very sight of those words.

What does this tell us about how society views the feminine? It suggests women are valued for their perceived utilitarian value, not their true value. This is a gigantic problem of perception which can only exist as long as human beings (particularly men) have not yet integrated and learned to value their own I-F. If they did, women, the harbingers of I-F, would be better understood, valued for their real potential, and treated as equals, not hand-maidens who exist for the sake of convenience.

UN worldwide statistics state:

- Up to 7 in 10 women around the world experience physical and/or sexual violence during their lives
- As many as one in four women experience physical or sexual violence during pregnancy
- 603 million women live in countries where domestic violence is not considered a crime

What does this rampant violence say about how women are honored and valued in society? Surely this could only happen – and then be made a "woman's issue" - in a society that is massively oriented toward the masculine.

6. Rape culture

According to studies by the US Centers for Disease Control and Prevention (2011), one in five American women will experience rape at some point during their lives (47). The actual percentage may be worse because rape is the most under-reported crime; 63% of sexual assaults are not reported to police (48).

The college rape crisis is a disturbing feature of modern campus life. A 2015 study by the Association of American Universities surveyed more than 150,000 students in 27 college campuses, including most of the Ivy League (49).

It confirms a shocking statistic: 23% of female students indicated that they experienced some form of unwanted sexual contact. This ranged from unwanted kissing to touching, to rape, either by force or while the women were incapacitated because of alcohol and drugs.

In war-torn countries rape is an epidemic. In the Democratic Republic of Congo estimates are that 200 000 women were raped during armed conflict between 1993 and 2003. The rape continues long after the war ended (50).

Sexual violence against girls is also prevalent. In the United States, 83 percent of girls aged 12 to 16 experience some form of sexual harassment in public schools (51).

UN statistics show that 120 million girls worldwide (slightly more than one in 10) have experienced forced sexual intercourse or other sexual acts at some point in their lives (52).

What does this tell us about society's treatment of the feminine? It suggests that women have a utilitarian value; they are things to be used for convenience and pleasure.

With excuses like "boys will be boys" the violation of women could only happen in an unbalanced society that has almost completely lost touch with the feminine.

7. Child Brides

One third of girls in developing countries are married before the age of 18 and one in nine is married before the age of 15 (53).

Pregnancy is consistently among the leading causes of death for girls ages 15 to 19 worldwide.

Being a child bride is a form of sexual violence and occurs mostly in South Asia (31.1 million) and Sub-Saharan Africa (14.1 million) (54).

Child brides typically show signs symptomatic of sexual abuse and post-traumatic stress disorder: feelings of hopelessness, helplessness and severe depression (53).

There are no words to describe the unbelievable suffering girls experience merely for the sexual pleasure of their husbands. This is truly a case of rampant I-M: "my needs at all costs." What does this violation say about how the needs of the feminine are taken into account?

8. *Female genital mutilation (FGM)*

The UN estimates that between 130 and 140 million girls and women alive today have undergone FGM, mainly in Africa and some Middle Eastern countries (54).

Three million girls a year are thought to be at risk of female genital mutilation (54). Procedures are carried out on girls between the ages of 0 and 15.

This unspeakably cruel act is motivated by cultural norms intended to control women by keeping girls "chaste", reducing female libido and discouraging women from having "illicit" sexual intercourse (55).

As recently as December 2012 the UN adopted its first resolution to eliminate FGM.

What does this societal norm found in certain parts of the world reveal about the rights of men vs. those of women? This attempt to control women is certainly not applied equally to men. What passes for a "traditional cultural practice" is really the workings of a society ruled by rampant, unbalanced I-M.

9. *Female gendercide*

Perhaps no other cultural practice demonstrates a clearer preference for the masculine over the feminine than the practice of female gendercide. This involves aborting or killing female infants and young girls because of a cultural preference for having boys.

One UN estimate is that 200 million women are missing in the world today due to selective abortion, abandonment or gross neglect of girl children (56). The worst offenders are China (66 million women missing) and India (43 million women missing). However, this practice is also carried out in many countries across South and East Asia, Western Asia, North Africa, Sub-Saharan Africa and Eastern Europe.

In China the birth rate is so skewed that approximately 100 girls are born to every 118 boys. Because of gendercide China now has an estimated 37 million more men than women. As a result of excess males in this population, human trafficking and sexual slavery are on the rise not only in China but also in surrounding countries (57).

Alarmingly, but perhaps not surprisingly, China also has the highest female suicide rate in the world. The U.S. State Department China Human Rights Report indicates that the number of female suicides has risen in recent years from 500 women per day to 590 (57).

10. Unequal access to education

Girls are still burdened with unequal access to education in both primary school and high school in most developing countries in the world. This cause was dramatically highlighted by Pakistani activist and 2014 Nobel Peace prize winner Malala Yousafzai.

As recently as 2015, approximately 70% of countries have achieved parity in primary school education and 50% in lower secondary education. In 2013, an estimated 60 million primary school and lower middle school age girls were out of school.

According to the World Bank - when it comes to the gender gap in high school education - the worst performing nations are in Sub-Saharan Africa and South Asia where the ratio of female to male high school graduates varies from around 25% to about 85%. Within these countries on average, a boy remains 1.55 times more likely than a girl to complete secondary school (58).

This leaves millions of girls and women vulnerable for the rest of their lives.

Conversely, the World Bank points out that an extra year of secondary school increases a girl's potential income by 15 to 25% and each year extra of a mother's schooling reduces infant mortality by 5 to 10% (59).

When girls have access to education it helps break the cycle of poverty. Educated women are less likely to marry early or be forced into marriage; less likely to die in childbirth; more likely to have healthy children; and are more likely to promote the education of their own children (60).

Thus, a positive ripple effect continues for generations to come. What does it tell us that girls are still denied their rights to education far more than boys? What does it tell us about how we value the feminine?

11. Feminization of poverty

The United Nations reported in 1997 that 70 percent of 1.3 billion people in poverty worldwide are women. (61)

According to the UN, women living in poverty are often denied access to critical resources such as credit, land and inheritance (62). Caught in the cycle of poverty, women lack access to resources and services to change their situation.

Another factor is that women's labor goes unrewarded and unrecognized. A WHO and UNICEF study shows that women and girls are 75% of household water collectors (63). The implications are that in sub-Saharan Africa, rural women collectively spend about 40 billion hours a year fetching water – equivalent to a year's labor for the entire workforce of France (64).

All this work and no income to show for it!

As the Special Rapporteur on Extreme Poverty and Human Rights has said, these heavy and unequal care and domestic responsibilities are a major barrier to gender equality and in many cases condemn women to poverty.

If rural women had equal access to productive resources, agricultural yields would rise, and there would be 100 million to 150 million fewer hungry people (64).

12. Attacks on gays and transsexuals

Hate crimes against gays and transsexuals uncover the belief that adhering to the gender binary is the only acceptable way for men and women to be. The attack on a gay night club in Orlando, Florida on June 12 2016 that left 49 people dead and 53 injured, is one example.

The 1999 movie *Boys Don't Cry* portrayed the vicious attack of a young woman for exploring her transsexual identity by dressing up like a man and falling in love with a woman.

Sadly, violence is aimed at gays, lesbians, bisexuals and transgender people just for being gender non-conforming.

Within this group of non-conformists, violence is disproportionately aimed at gay men and transsexual women (65). What do these two groups have in common? Both represent men who have veered into "feminine territory." Gay men are more in touch with their feminine side than most men are and transsexual women have gone as far as to identify fully with their feminine side.

This disproportionate targeting suggests that as a society we are not only intolerant of gender non-conformity in general, but particularly of the idea of men integrating their feminine side.

This issue underscores the imbalance this book seeks to expose: a widespread devaluing of I-F.

13. Religious oppression of the feminine

This is a big topic so we will only focus on one aspect. Major western religions such as Christianity, Judaism and Islam created and maintain the myth that God is male. This is despite the Bible (Gen 1:27) stating:

So God created mankind in his own image, in the image of God he created them; male and female he created them.

If God created male and female in God's image, how can God be a "he"? This logic boggles the mind. It is one of the perversions of patriarchal thinking that occurred when sacred messages were reshaped into meanings that suited the status quo.

What does it say about society that its major religions do not consider women every bit as divine as men?

What is the likely impact when one half of society is depicted as "divine" and the other half as not? Could this contribute to the chronic low self-esteem and self-doubt commonly found in women? Might it have given an added excuse and justification for the abuse and subjugation of women over the centuries?

What does this "male divinity bias" reflect about the way the I-M and I-F are valued?

14. Sexual double standards

What double standards apply to the sexes?

An example is when assertive behavior is applauded in men, yet is labeled "bossy" or aggressive in women (66). This particular example could only exist in a society that still adheres to a gender binary.

In a society acknowledging that men and women have I-M and I-F, assertive behavior in women would simply be understood as "she's expressing an aspect of her I-M right now."

Another example is when having many sexual partners earns men the label of "stud" and women the label of "slut." Fortunately, these double standards are increasingly being called out with new terms like "man slut" appearing.

It might be tempting to think of these double standards being applied *by* men *to* women but this is not entirely true. One study shows that both men and women judge women more harshly for having sex on the first date or during the early stages of dating (67).

Nothing quite tops double standards as those imposed on women for adultery (68) in parts of the Middle East and North Africa.

In these countries women are stoned to death for the same "crime" that a man could just walk away from. Aside from the barbaric method of punishment itself, women are disproportionately targeted. A woman could be stoned at marriage just for not being a virgin. The same requirement does not apply to the man. On the other hand, if a man rapes a woman or takes her virginity he is not put to death; he is sentenced to marry the woman and pay money to her father. How would this be experienced from the woman's perspective? The woman's needs are violated twice with no recompense whatsoever and the offender gets off lightly.

A joint statement by the United Nations Working Group on discrimination against women in law and in practice states that: "Adultery as a criminal offence violates women's human rights" (68). The term "adultery" might even be applied loosely to exercise power over others, particularly women. Amnesty International has petitioned countries such as Iran to stop stoning and to remove any form of punishment by execution for adultery (69).

What does it tell us about the highly skewed way in which men and women are treated for the same sexual behavior? What does this tell us about how we value and respect the masculine and the feminine?

15. Misrepresentation and underrepresentation in movies

Women are often misrepresented by being portrayed as two-dimensional characters with no greater purpose than to be walking down the aisle with Mr Right. While women do tend to value relationships and are good at building them, this depiction robs them of being fully human with interests and ambitions of their own that go beyond marriage and domestic bliss.

Females are also grossly underrepresented in movies. A comprehensive study by the University of Southern California (USC) shows that out of 700 top grossing movies between 2007 and 2014, only 30% of speaking characters were female (70). Of the 700 movies, only 11% had gender-balanced casts.

Where have all the women gone?

The USC report shows that in 2014, no female actor over 45 years old performed a lead or co-lead role. This arguably demonstrates that women are viewed with *a narrow lens that focuses on young female sexuality* rather than for who they are: multifaceted individuals with a wide variety of strengths, talents and interests.

If women were widely understood to have this multitude of skills and capabilities, surely it would be no problem to depict them in strong leading roles? Would this defy the "sanctity" of the gender binary and the status quo?

I remember how I felt when it occurred to me that in *Finding Nemo (2003)*, the *highest selling DVD of all time*, the vast majority of characters in the movie are male. Two characters are female. One is Dory, the female fish who *seems to be free to swim around only because she has lost her memory.* What does this in itself tell us?

One other creature - a pink starfish - is female. Every other fish, sea creature or bird in the movie is male. The large flock of seagulls hanging out in Sydney Harbor is all male based on their clearly male voices.

A list of the movie credits shows that a whopping 2% of the characters are female. Where are the females? Or does this movie simply reflect a gender stereotype that assumes females are somewhere behind the scenes at home in the kitchen or tending to the young? As though that completely defines the female experience of life? What message does this send to the *billions of children* who have seen this movie?

When women are depicted in narrow and gender-stereotyped ways it not only misrepresents women but renders their true nature invisible. I would challenge the movie industry to start having fun with depicting women in multifaceted roles that go beyond gender stereotypes. It could open up a whole new genre particularly for female characters that are masculine-feminine balanced.

16. *Schools value math and science above creativity*

A subtler sign that we prefer I-M is that schools value math and science above creativity. This point was amply highlighted in one of the most popular TED talks of all time: a humorous talk by Ken Robinson (71) titled "Do schools kill creativity?"

Similarly, CNN host Fareed Zakaria wrote: "In defense of a liberal education." He challenges the notion that only technical training is valuable. He exposes state governors for refusing to spend taxpayer money to fund the liberal arts in college campuses. A liberal education, he argues, "provides the foundation for finding your voice, writing, speaking your mind and learning." Surely this holds value.

What is not usually openly said is that these creative and enriching subjects including art, literature, history, philosophy, psychology, women's studies and English are reminiscent of feminine energy, whereas math, science and technical training are reminiscent of masculine energy.

What does this show us about the way we value I-F and I-M?

17. Default male pronouns

Many people use male pronouns by default when referring to people, birds, animals or fish.

We talk about the views of "the man in the street" as though the default person is male or "businessmen" as though all entrepreneurs are men.

We see a squirrel bounding up a tree with an acorn and we exclaim to our child "Look at the squirrel. *He's* got an acorn." Soon our children echo this bias: "Look at the bird, mommy! He's flying away."

What are the implications? When we make "he" the default, "she" becomes relegated to "other." Isn't patriarchy precisely the notion that masculine is "standard" and feminine is "other"? Clearly this makes no sense given the reality that the universe is a perfect balance of I-M and I-F. If anything, females slightly outnumber males in any species.

How is this implied invisibility and irrelevance of the feminine likely to impact young girls (and boys) when their minds are being shaped? What are we educating ourselves and others to believe when we're reinforcing the idea that the feminine doesn't count? Once again, what does this tendency show us about how we acknowledge and respect the existence of the I-M and I-F?

The 17 examples cited above are not a comprehensive list of the issues. We haven't addressed female reproductive rights which includes the right to choose, nor female sexual slavery, honor killings and other issues. Nor have we covered factory farming and animal testing, which are not obviously about the oppression of the feminine, but they do represent the outcome of rampant, unbalanced I-M calling the shots. The animals represent I-F in the sense that they are at the receiving end of what is meted out to them.

By now you should have a good sense of where we are as a society today and what your answer is to the question: "Aren't we balanced enough?"

Times are changing but as a society we have a way to go before we can truly say that we value and appreciate I-M and I-F equally.

Some people ask: But what can I do? I'm just one person.

The greatest gift you can give is cultivating an equal appreciation for your I-M and I-F by bringing them to balance within yourself. By doing this you are "being the change you wish to see" and becoming a role model for others as well as giving yourself an opportunity to thrive.

Why is the feminine undervalued?

Undervaluing the feminine is the cause of enormous suffering in the world.

Why is the feminine so undervalued? I do not believe that people are inherently evil. So why is it such a widespread tendency across time and space?

Two reasons emerge.

1. The feminine is not well understood

Being the subtler of the two complementary opposite energies; the feminine is less immediately obvious.

By contrast, I-M is more visible, more tangible. The connection between I-M inputs and results is obvious. Consider the connection between hard work and achievement.

The American Dream is based on the concept of prosperity through hard work.

I-F means working smarter, which would bring the American Dream into fruition more quickly, with less effort.

But I-F is subtler, more hidden from view.

Consider the Law of Attraction - a largely internal process for getting results without relying much on action. According to the Esther and Jerry Hicks (72), when the Law of Attraction is utilized properly, action is a tiny fraction of the process. It is a process that involves working with feelings, energy levels and clear intentions. To the outside world this entire process is invisible. The outcomes may be visible but the process is invisible.

Someone in the process of using the Law of Attraction could appear to be inactive, just sitting about. Yet, nothing could be further from the truth.

The subtlety of I-F is something we need to learn to recognize, appreciate and utilize. Until we do, it bypasses the intellect.

It is easier to believe in the tangible: to get what I want I need to do this, go there, work hard and struggle. As though "real life" is what's outside us.

A common belief is: "unless I can "see, touch and feel it, it doesn't exist." Or it isn't valid. Isn't this how mainstream Western thinking has dismissed meditation and natural remedies for so long?

There are many other examples of how I-M is more visible, more tangible than I-F. Try "going to war" vs "sitting around a table to find a peaceful solution" or perhaps "asserting my point of view" vs "listening to the other person's point of view."

By its very nature I-M is visible, in-your-face stuff. I-F is subtle and less visible. Our mistake is assuming that this makes it less powerful.

When society goes through a patriarchal era, the relative elusiveness and quiet power of the feminine lends itself to being misunderstood and even feared. After all there is nothing so feared as the unknown - especially when deep down we know she is powerful in her own right.

Fear and suspicion of the feminine means valuable feminine capabilities are misinterpreted, misunderstood and unnecessarily vilified.

The feminine is commonly mistaken for:

- Weakness: It is thought that strength and power are shown in visible displays such as in combat or sports. Sports men and military men are often jokingly referred to by the coach as "ladies" until they have "proved themselves" worthy as men. This one-sided view does not appreciate the psychological strength and courage it takes to remain loving, forgiving, nurturing and considerate of others' needs while facing challenges that cannot be overcome with might. Yet this inner strength is a hallmark of mature I-F.
- Mystery and intangibles: Intuition and "following your heart" rather than tangible, familiar ways such as the use of logic and verifiable data as ways to make decisions and solve problems

- Giving power away: Diplomacy, yielding or compromise are considered "weakness" as opposed to the "strength" of a "winning is everything" mentality.
- Indecision: I-F considers a wider and more complex range of variables that take longer-term outcomes into account. The decision may take longer because of these many factors, but the quality of the decision is far superior. It is well-known that female board members function best when they have time to consider an issue, so that they can take the complexities into account and weigh them up. This is how the best business decisions are made.
- Power and evil: women were burned at the stake as witches because of their intuitive gifts and abilities to work with subtle forces. In reality, our intuition can save us from disastrous decisions. It can literally save our lives or save years of unhappiness. The Law of Attraction utilizes subtle forces that are universally available so that we can co-create the reality we desire. Creative visualization, meditation, learning to harness the power of intentionality – these are all aspects of I-F. These bring incredible value into our lives. Their power comes from the ability to master the subtle.

How much better off would we be if society, including ourselves, could come to understand and appreciate I-F?

2. Unbalanced feminine is easily taken advantage of

By "unbalanced feminine" I mean a woman who identifies with her feminine side but has not sufficiently enlivened her I-M in order to balance out particular tendencies. This imbalance can occur in some men too, but it is predominantly an issue experienced by women who are unbalanced.

What happens next?

The innate generosity and openness of the I-F is her frame of reference. It feels most natural to her. The following tendencies are easy to take advantage of:

- A desire to please
- A desire to nurture
- A desire to maintain relationships even at a high cost to oneself
- A desire to be of service
- A tendency toward sensitivity
- A tendency to yield or compromise rather than fight

Rather than being valued, these qualities are often abused. The first part of this chapter made that clear.

Who takes advantage of unbalanced I-F? It is those with unbalanced I-M. This does not occur with men or women who are balanced.

Being balanced necessarily makes it almost impossible to try to benefit from the suffering of others. The misuse of the feminine only occurs with people who strongly identify with their I-M and are out of touch with their I-F.

Here is why: *unbalanced masculine* has a strong tendency to put its own needs first even if it comes at the expense of others.

It is more than just taking the feminine for granted. It is a willingness to keep her in a subservient or disadvantaged position so that more of the "good stuff" – money, time, energy, relaxation – can be kept for oneself. It comes down to doing this "because I can."

Being balanced is the only way out because it means "even if I can, I would not want to."

Up until recently feminine energy has been equated with women (as part of the gender binary) and has been relegated to the domestic sphere where it has conveniently served the interests of men wishing to focus on developing careers and being out in the world.

As we emerge from the patriarchal era, giving up this "privilege" would mean taking personal responsibility and playing fair.

The best way to get there is to acknowledge, understand and enliven the feminine within ourselves.

The global imbalance is now urgently calling for feminine energy to go beyond being confined to the domestic sphere and be restored *in the world* – at the decision tables of government and business where the lives of millions are affected. Families and communities will always need feminine energy to be the loving glue that holds it all together – and in the new era, this will come from both men and women.

Right now the world needs balanced women and men need to express the wisdom and power of the feminine at the top echelons of business, education, social and government institutions.

It is time to stop taking advantage of the generosity of the feminine for selfish gain and instead free it to be used at institutional levels for the greater good.

Imbalance as a source of suffering

This chapter was intended to provide perspective on the question of how balanced we are as a global society.

It is empowering to put things into perspective, particularly to see that the painful imbalances we see "out there in the world" ultimately come down to the same thing: an imbalance between I-M and I-F. This is its ultimate source.

This is why I can reasonably say: "show me a problem, and I'll show you a masculine-feminine imbalance."

Another way to put this is: the suffering we see in the world today – the state of the world – is as it is due a widespread misunderstanding of the *Law of Balance*. There may be individuals who get it but as a whole society does not understand that the *Law of Balance* applies, and that if we want function well – to thrive – as individuals and as a society we need to honor masculine and feminine energy equally and bring them into balance.

Whether we are considering work-life balance issues in our personal lives or the global undermining of women and men in touch with their feminine side, much of the suffering in the world comes down to the same cause: *a preference for I-M over I-F.*

This brings us full circle. If we want to see the feminine restored to her rightful place as an equally loved and respected presence in the world, we need to create that same balance and equality within ourselves. This frees us and the world to thrive.

CHAPTER 8

How Does the Gender Binary Affect Us?

"Boys don't cry."
"Women shouldn't express anger."
"Men don't cook."
"Women don't mow the lawn."

These are a few examples of the gender binary, placing people into gendered categories. But how does it play out and is there a relationship to patriarchy?

So far we have seen the evidence of a global imbalance favoring the masculine at the expense of the feminine. While there are exceptions, we are still challenged by a collective imbalance toward I-M.

This chapter explores the gender binary. It is one of the greatest obstacles to inner balance. Those wishing to become balanced will benefit from knowing its pitfalls and how to sidestep it.

What is the gender binary?

The gender binary is a pervasive belief that we can be one of two things: masculine or feminine, but not both.

In essence it equates men with I-M and women with I-F. There is little or no room for overlap.

Jennifer Siebel Newsom, director of *The Mask You Live In*, describes it this way (73):

> *Around the world, what you're finding is that there's a lot of value in cultures, in America in particular, placed on masculine-associated attributes like dominance, control, and aggression — at the expense of more feminine-associated attributes like empathy, care, compassion, and collaboration.*
>
> *Boys are socialized right out of the womb, often unconsciously, to think that there is a hierarchy called the gender binary, that the masculine is more valuable than the feminine. And as early as four, they are being told to be dominant, to repress emotions, to not cry, to disassociate from the natural self.*

When President Obama was seen shedding a tear on television (74) while lamenting the death of young children due to gun violence, the US media went ablaze about "what this really means."

Members of media outlets and Republican Party members mocked his behavior, calling into question his strength and fitness to be a leader. This is a classic example of the gender binary.

The message is clear: "Men don't cry."

Much of this conditioning is so deeply ingrained that it is subconscious; until we cultivate awareness, it remains invisible because we're so steeped in it. Like a fish in water we continue to bask in the familiarity of the status quo, unaware that it represents a *particular* worldview.

Comedian and social activist Sam Killerman summed up his own feelings about the gender binary during a TED Talk (75):

> *Our understanding of gender as binary is sick. And to make someone confined to one of two options when in their minds they know that that role isn't for them.... I know myself better than you could ever know me and who*

are you to say what's healthy when your idea of health is destroying a part of me?

Sam Killerman's message could not be clearer. As a society we need to be aware of this, because until we do so, we run the risk of being part of the problem.

How does society promote it?

Here are some examples - by no means comprehensive - of how the gender binary is perpetuated. It starts the moment we are born and continues for the rest of our lives.

- Newborn babies are traditionally given pink or blue clothes depending on their gender.
- From a young age, children are exposed to toy shops with gendered aisles with starkly different messages of what is considered "normal" and "desirable." Girls get pink aisles with soft cuddly toys, tea sets, doll houses and baby dolls. Boys get blue aisles with guns, action men, cars, trucks, chemistry sets, puzzles and mechanical toys. Even though girls could arguably veer into the boy's aisle or vice versa, many simply would not. The pressure to be "normal" is just too great. Toys are more divided by gender now than they were fifty years ago (76).
- Children and teenagers are daily at the receiving end of conditioning from peers, elders, schools, religion, and the media.
    - Girls get the message that their role is to nurture others and express themselves within the domestic sphere and that they are "not suited" to pursuits that require leadership, math, logical thinking and spatial awareness.
    - Boys learn that it is OK to be assertive to the point of aggression to get their needs met, that they are strong and smart enough to learn about mechanical toys and spatial awareness.

- - Thus a "macho, me-first culture" is instilled in boys from the outset and a "subservient, you-first culture" is instilled in girls.
  - Later during teenage years this foundation develops into "sexting", cell phone texting in which teenage girls understand that it is "absolutely normal" to make themselves available visually or sexually to boys, the purpose being to satisfy boys' desires and to feel wanted. Boys, conditioned to be assertive and gung-ho, may exploit this and take it as far as they can go.
  - Later in high school and college the "macho, winner-takes-all culture" contributes to the rape epidemic on campuses.

- Adults continue to be pressured into the gender binary. One example is how men and women are portrayed in the media. Social activist Jennifer Siebel Newsom created a grassroots movement #Askhermore for journalists to ask female actors, politicians and businesswomen more than just the usual questions about physical appearance. It challenges journalists to ask about their successes, their insights and their future plans, questions routinely asked of their male counterparts.
- Religion has for centuries conditioned men and women to have different roles and privileges. This is not entirely surprising given that most modern day religions were formed during the rise of patriarchy and are built upon values that emphasize rules and dogma, differentiation, hierarchy and exclusivity.

Ironically, considering that feminine receptivity and sensitivity is what connects us intuitively with the Divine, it is mind-boggling that women, the harbingers of the feminine, have for millennia been kept out of positions of spiritual authority in the church. Throughout history nuns were largely relegated to serving the male priesthood, who in turn could serve a male God directly.

Women have been ordained as priests in some churches such as the Quaker movement since the 1800s. Since the 1990s this movement has gained momentum with mainstream churches such as the Church of

England ordaining women priests since 1992 (77). This church saw its first female Bishop in 2015. Female Rabbis were first admitted in 1985. The Catholic Church remains officially closed to women priests.

- Some Eastern meditative spiritual traditions, whose primary purpose is to assist people on their journey to enlightenment, are also entrenched in the gender binary.
    - In a Vedic tradition that provides a specific meditation technique for millions around the world, women are barred from positions of authority beyond a certain point. Yet, the guru is considered to be enlightened.
    - Samantha, a friend had spent three months training to become a meditation teacher in this tradition. After her teacher training she and the other female graduates posed for an official group photo. After the photo was submitted to headquarters, it was returned with a terse reply. The group was instructed to re-take the photo. Why? Because one woman (Samantha) was wearing slacks *and not a skirt*. It was simply the fact that she was wearing pants, which is deemed "for men only."

- Women's and men's clothing reflects the gender binary. A few years ago my husband and I got scooters. While shopping for a biker's jacket, I discovered that only men's jackets were fitted with protective armor - designed to shield the body in key areas in the event of an accident. Women's jackets were shapely and pretty but there was not one option with protective armor! The message is: as a woman your looks are more important than your personal safety – even in a potentially dangerous pursuit.

One last example: Designers and manufacturers of female underwear traditionally used thin elastic bands in the seams around the hips and legs during the 80s. While this may look dainty, when it comes to comfort and health it makes no sense. High school science tells us that Pressure = Force / Area. The narrower the elastic band, the higher the pressure on the skin. This results in the constriction of blood flow which is uncomfortable and unhealthy.

The message here is: as a woman your looks are more important than your comfort and health. This message extends to the corsets worn by women in Victorian times and to the high heeled shoes of today. I breathed a sigh of relief in the 90s when Jockey came out with a range of comfortable and attractive underwear for women and soon other clothing manufacturers followed suit.

These are just some of the ways in which the gender binary plays out by keeping men and women in separate boxes based on gender stereotypical ideas about who we are.

How we unknowingly perpetuate it

During some point in our upbringing the conditioning from the outside world becomes internalized.

At that point we no longer need society to tell us how to behave: we become our own enforcers and we put on a show so that we can fit in.

Pressure to conform has us monitoring: am I behaving like a man is supposed to? Am I behaving the way a woman should? Is it OK to wear this? Is it OK to say that?

As we grow up we pass on these internalized beliefs to younger generations by way of what we say and do. And so the unconscious cycle of conditioning continues.

The outcome

With men shunted into their masculine side and women shunted into their feminine side (although with mixed messages) we are perpetuating a society of two halves.

I-M and I-F are both fundamentally good and are absolutely necessary for us to thrive. They are both necessary for us to become self-realized, enlightened souls. But when developed in isolation without the perspective of the other embodied *within oneself*, they potentially become toxic.

What hypermasculine creates

What is hypermasculine energy? It is one step beyond excessive I-M, the kind that leads us to work too hard without a break. This is taking it to the next level and it is gender-specific: it is experienced by men who buy into the gender binary.

It is a tendency to exude an aggressive, outward-facing energy with a me-first attitude, a need to "win" and a lack of empathy for others. This is the nature of I-M when little or none of the complementary opposite energy is present to balance and guide it toward more fruitful outcomes.

In chapter two I-M was defined in its core as *outward, active and differentiating*. There is absolutely nothing wrong with these qualities. By themselves they are neutral and when used appropriately they are enormously positive.

However, when men become hypermasculine, which is the outcome of the gender binary on men, they have no other frame of reference but I-M. The world is seen through a masculine lens in terms of "winners and losers", "us and them", "fight or flight" as well as other dichotomies. Hierarchy becomes super-important. The use of might and aggression are seen as "manly."

During the colorful 2016 US presidential election race it became apparent that most of the Republican candidates (there were 11 to begin with) wanted to increase the already massive military budget – which is larger than the *next seven countries put together*. They also intimated going to war in the Middle East at the drop of a hat. President Obama was called "weak" and a "lame duck president" for seeking diplomatic solutions in the Middle East. Then-presidential-candidate Ted Cruz advocated "carpet bombing ISIS into oblivion" (78) and Donald Trump declared "I would bomb the shit out of them" (79). This is hypermasculine.

Given the "hypermasculine ideal" as a yardstick for men to measure themselves by, it is not surprising that men perpetuate most of the physical violence in the world. In the US men are responsible for over 90 percent of all murders (80). Whites and blacks commit these crimes proportionately to their population.

Mass shootings are a well-known phenomenon in the US, but what is perhaps less known is that gender plays a role. One statistic shows that in school shootings girls are twice as likely to be targeted (81). One theme is that male shooters are perhaps bent on proving their masculinity as a "beta-male" in a world where "alpha-males" get all the girls and where they have felt let down by women.

90% of murder-suicides are perpetrated by men and 78% of those killed are women. These are disturbing trends especially since the gender angle typically receives little to no coverage after a shooting. Media coverage tends to fixate on gun control while missing a crucial piece of the puzzle.

However, the media – largely owned and run by men – wouldn't think to ask these questions being part of the dominant group, which tends not to ask questions that might uncover its own system of power abuse and privilege.

Men with hypermasculine show an inability to deal with their emotions and to know when to stop. They seem to know one thing: how to assert their needs and get them met through aggression.

What hyperfeminine energy creates

Similarly, hyperfeminine energy is a step beyond excessive feminine, and is gender-specific: it is experienced by women who buy into the gender binary.

When I-F is unbalanced, an individual becomes dominated by an overly-giving, timid, martyr-like energy. It seeks to build relationships at all costs. Consider the phrase "hell hath no fury like a woman scorned." It suggests the most painful experience for a woman is to be cast out of a relationship.

This need is so high that it easily veers toward self-abandonment in order to take care of others and in turn, be valued. This is where "martyrdom" comes in.

While it may seem noble on some level, it is a function of the ego because it is about playing a certain role with an expected payoff such as safety, security and feeling needed.

When its needs aren't met it can also resort to violence, but usually in subtler ways such as emotional manipulation, passive-aggressive behavior and guilt tripping.

The hyperfeminine also does not know when to stop. For this to happen, a woman needs her I-M to assert itself, stand up and create healthy boundaries.

In a world that worships progress and outer forms of achievement, many women from Baby Boomers and beyond are more likely to be a mixture of I-M and I-F, not purely hyperfeminine individuals.

Often, women may be overly connected to their I-M in some areas such as work, yet in other areas, such as relationships and the home, they may be more prone to being hyperfeminine. This is more balanced than being entirely hyperfeminine but it is still a way off from true inner balance.

The outcome: suffering

It all comes together in predictable suffering: due to the dominant nature of hypermasculine energy and the submissive, overly generous nature of hyperfeminine energy, the relationship-focused female ends up in a subservient role for the convenience of the outward-facing, self-entitled male.

It may be tempting to think of this as happening only in developing countries but this is not so. As shown in chapter 7, women all over the world still carry the burden of "the second shift" – coming home from work only to have the lion's share of responsibilities in the home. Women all over the world contend with the gender pay gap, misrepresentation in the media and the default use of male pronouns. These examples reflect the expectation that women should be generous and selfless to the point of self-sacrifice.

Yet, as chapter 7 shows, there are many – and more intense – examples of the imbalance that unfairly burdens women, ranging from discrimination to violence. Each of these examples reflects the dominant, self-serving nature of the hypermasculine at the expense of the feminine.

This is the outcome of the gender binary. Interestingly, this also describes patriarchy. It seems the two are inextricably related.

The cause: the gender binary

We have come full circle. The greatest source of our problems in the world today is the imbalance caused by patriarchy as shown in the previous chapter. The greatest source of this imbalance is the gender binary (this chapter).

Social pressure for men and women to operate as two separate halves creates hypermasculinity and hyperfemininity, which is the source of imbalance. Due to the nature of each of these extremes, a vicious cycle ensues creating oppressors and victims.

It's sad that we as a society continue to perpetuate the gender binary as though it is a good thing. We keep conditioning children and each other into the gender binary, yet this is precisely what creates the imbalance that leads to all this suffering.

We are doing this to ourselves. Have we not made the connection?

We seem to give in to "the way it has always been," not quite able to articulate what an alternative such as inner balance looks like.

Yet, as we are entering the new era, life will begin to require more from us. *What may have made sense before will simply not work in the future.* The sexual division of labor and roles may have made sense at a time when survival was our greatest imperative. Men went out to hunt and women stayed home to gather food and raise children.

Not so today.

We no longer live in a society whose highest ideal is survival and defining ourselves by predefined roles. We are further along in Maslow's hierarchy of human needs (82). We live in a time where individuals can become self-actualized, and give expression to their unique, individual potential.

Moreover, right now the world needs feminine energy to come forward and be expressed – not only at home – but at the decision tables of government, business, research and education.

To achieve this, we must free ourselves from the gender binary. Instead, we need to embrace *gender fluidity*, another way of referring to "inner balance."

This is being in touch with both sides of ourselves and being able to dial these up or down as needed in the moment.

Are men even more subject to the gender binary?

Social pressure to conform to the gender binary applies to both genders but is arguably harder on men.

In the West, women have made strides to integrate their masculine side since entering the workplace *en masse* during and after WWII. Working women must necessarily get in touch with certain aspects of their masculine side: having a bias for action, focusing on tasks and outcomes, cultivating a certain professional demeanor, working with hierarchy, learning self-promotion, cultivating assertiveness and being financially self-sufficient.

Men on the whole have generally been slower to integrate their feminine side. However, there are growing numbers of men who are bucking the status quo and are making strides to become whole, balanced individuals.

Masculinity in a patriarchal world

When considering masculinity in a patriarchal world it may be harder for men to shift toward balance because in that context *masculinity is winning*. In the new era, masculinity will be *winning with*. It will include achievement and getting things done – but in ways that are inclusive, that are genuinely, and more widely, beneficial.

Patriarchy has sidelined men into an impossible "ideal" of the individualist who must constantly demonstrate his strength, stamina, his ability to "take charge" and have all the answers.

This is exhausting, not to mention unrealistic.

It leaves very little space for anything else – notably the feminine side – to come in.

Jennifer Siebel Newsom, director of *The Mask You Live In*, explores how America's narrow definition of masculinity is harming boys, men, and society at large (83).

> *Pressured by the media, their peer group, and even the adults in their lives, our protagonists confront messages encouraging them to disconnect from their emotions,*

> *devalue authentic friendships, objectify and degrade women, and resolve conflicts through violence. These gender stereotypes interconnect with race, class, and circumstance, creating a maze of identity issues boys and young men must navigate to become "real" men.*

This relentless pressure to be a "real man" is likely to hook most men in some way at different levels of conscious awareness. This leaves a conundrum for men: how can I integrate my softer, feminine side without ending up looking weak and pathetic?

The first step is getting to know what the feminine *really* is. I-F is *anything but* weak and pathetic.

When I discovered the difference between true I-F and the socialized concept of the feminine, it opened things for me particularly when my I-M was predominant. Once I realized what the feminine really is, and what it could bring into my life, I wanted it. It was easy to welcome it.

Fear of change and loss of power

Maintaining gender stereotypes may preserve a sense of entitlement and privilege for men, but it comes at a high cost: a lack of internal and external peace and harmony.

Internally, it is a high price to pay over time because the soul gets eroded.

Externally, it is a high price to pay because deep down one knows that others are suffering as a result. As we all know, guilt is not a good feeling. This awareness may in turn set up a vicious cycle in which it becomes easier to stuff one's feelings down and adhere even more to the familiar hypermasculinity.

An act of surrender is likely to be an essential ingredient for men to transcend the hypermasculine ideal. This is not surrendering to an "other." It is surrendering the grip of the ego and its self-entitlement for the guidance of the soul. This enables us to become more fully human and truly effective. It is surrendering the need to dominate or make use of others "just because I can." This is liberating.

Riding on privilege may keep life predictable, controllable and convenient, but it comes at a huge cost.

Men fare better in women-friendly societies

In countries that have made strides to let go of the gender binary and its close cousin patriarchy, life is better for everyone.

The Global Gender Gap Index compiled by the World Economic Forum ranks 145 countries according to how well their female talent pool is leveraged based on economic, educational, health-based and political indicators.

The 2015 Global Gender Gap Index (84) identifies the top 10 women-friendly countries as: Iceland, Norway, Finland, Sweden, Ireland, Rwanda, Philippines, Switzerland, Slovenia and New Zealand.

Studies have shown that everybody fares better in women-friendly countries.

In an article called "Feminism's social side effects" (2011) Hank Pellisier (85), Managing Director of the Institute for Ethics and Emerging Technologies writes that women-friendly countries fare well in these areas: male longevity is higher and GDP per capita is higher. Moreover, these are among the happiest, most peaceful, most democratic countries of the world. They are also among the most non-religious countries in the world.

He writes:

> *Feminism, aka "Women's Equality", is the glue that unites all positive characteristics. Advancing the status of women guides a population towards a progressive, transhumanist society that offers wealth, health, peace, joy, and open-mindedness.*

In short: everybody wins. A world made better for women is a better world for everyone.

CHAPTER 9

Case Study – Paulo

Paulo is a 47-year old business entrepreneur. At the age of 25 he was managing various business interests and subsequently launched what later became a multimillion dollar franchise network.

Paulo's journey illustrates much of what was discussed in the previous chapter. It provides a real-life example of a man who was raised strictly according to the gender binary, and how it shaped him as a human being.

It also provides insight into what changed his trajectory and enabled him to awaken his I-F and how this positively transformed his life.

Childhood conditioning

Paulo was raised in a Portuguese-South African family and a culture he describes as having patriarchal values.

> *I was strictly raised to develop my male energy. There were a lot of expectations around who you were supposed to be.*
>
> *My Dad, a greengrocer, pushed it quite strongly. He had a clear idea of who his son needed to be. It had to be male, masculine energy. I was meant to be the provider, the role model, the worker.*

I had to work hard. I didn't necessarily need to study: I needed to be a good businessman. My Dad used to arrive with his truck and I had to unload the vegetables. If the other boys could unload three bags of potatoes at a time, I had to unload four. You had to do more. That is how you showed you were a man.

It was made very clear to me that expressing my feminine side was not appropriate. Creativity was for girls. It was frowned upon if I painted. The idea was "Isn't there something better you could spend your time on, like in the shop?" It was real, and we grew up with it.

If I cried, I got a smack because "boys don't cry." It was unacceptable, a sign of weakness.

Paulo alludes to his upbringing which clearly illustrates the gender binary. How did this shape him?

Looking back, I had become cold, calculating and a real capitalist, or as I realize today, an "unconscious capitalist". Everything had a price tag. It was all about money, profit, power, status and having material things.

As an adult I was an academic bully: I had to win. Things had to be my way. I was very assertive. If I didn't like what somebody else was doing, I let them know about it. As a businessman I was quite autocratic: "We don't pay you to give suggestions."

My masculine energy was given too much prominence.

I looked at things from the perspective of right and wrong. There was a lot of judgment.

I was very "homophobic" around feminine energy. As soon as a person expressed a delicate or softer side of themselves, that was a sign of weakness. Back to my father, even if we got a dog and the dog showed delicate tendencies – if it didn't bark – it wasn't a dog worth having.

Interestingly I was always in conflict with it. It's as if I knew it wasn't right. I was always lectured on the dangers of expressing my feminine side. That side was seen as weakness. Its purpose was supporting and validating male energy.

In our house if a guy spoke softly or showed emotion and was soft or had empathy, he was called a "paneleiro", a derogatory classification for "gay". I avoided gay men, lesbians and trans people. In primary school there was a boy with a gay orientation. In my mind he was "weakness" so I could justify putting a dead frog in his pencil case because he "deserved it."

Catalyst for change

Then an unexpected event changed Paulo's life.

It happened when I was about 25 years old. For security I had arranged to have a boom put in our street. My neighbor refused so I barged over and banged on her door. I wanted to say "how dare you?" Later we become good friends.

This woman was the deputy editor of a national newspaper, not a pushover by any means. After seeing what appeared to be a massage table in her home I discovered that she was a Reiki master. I had no idea what Reiki was. She said: "You need to balance your energies." I avoided her for three months but then finally had the Reiki session.

> *While performing the Reiki session on me, I noticed that she went to the bathroom every few minutes to wash her hands. "What's the matter?" I asked.*
>
> *She replied, "I have never met anyone with so much energy in their head, and so little in the heart. Because of the work I'm doing with you, my hands heat up tremendously and I need to cool them off."*

Paulo's first thought was "oh, please."

> *Understanding how he might interpret this, she offered, "Next time it happens you can feel for yourself." A few minutes later she said "I'm going to put my hand on you but I'm warning you it's going to feel hot."*
>
> *When I say to you "I nearly jumped off the Reiki table" I'm not kidding. It felt like she took a hot iron and pressed it to my skin. I got the fright of my life. My mind couldn't wrap itself around this and make a logical story out of it. I just had to accept that there was this energy and something had happened. I couldn't argue with it.*
>
> *That was the turning point for me. My whole mindset changed. It was a life-changing event.*
>
> *She also said "Within a few days you are going to become very emotional." Lo and behold, three days later it washed over me. An ambulance sped past with its siren blaring and I broke down in an uncontrollable fit of emotion. To this day if I hear an ambulance siren or police siren, I get quietly tearful.*

As a result of the Reiki incident Paulo had some insights about himself.

> *When she said "there is no energy flowing from your head to your heart chakra" I understood it to be there is*

no energy flowing from the masculine side – the thinking, analytical side – to my heart, my feminine side.

For me it was real and true.

Thus began an inner journey and I said "Wait a minute, there is another side to me. There is this soft and loving side." Then I began to link that side to creativity, to these other things that I would previously have thought were trivial.

Life in masculine-only mode

I asked Paulo to reflect on what was missing from life when operating from I-M only.

What's missing from your life is life.

It's like I was a full-color HD television but I was operating on black and white settings. It still told the picture and conveyed the message. It did what it had to. It was functional. It could succeed and build a life and earn accolades, but it was only in black and white.

So for me when that other switch got turned on it was like I suddenly discovered: "Oh my God, you mean I can do my life in full color?! Wow!"

Then I had to consciously go on a journey to say "Ok, how do I play with color now? I don't really know how to play with color, I only know how to play with black and white, which is this masculine, male, logical, everything-must-make-sense world."

Balance has brought a lot of value into my life and I can honestly say I'm committed to it. It has since transformed

> *me at my core. It is hard to express in words how much it has changed my life.*

Cultivating his I-F

Aside from the Reiki incident and the opening it created in him, Paulo continued to find ways to embrace his I-F. He attended spiritual and metaphysical courses and learned a lot from the teacher. Eventually they became friends.

One day she said:

> *"You've got to make space for female energy in your life. You have to literally make space for it."*
>
> *I mulled it over. I started a journal and consciously started making space for the feminine.*

One of the ways Paulo made a shift was in his views about relationships.

> *I'd had relationships before, but they always served a purpose. They were like a utility. Yes, you need them but they had a purpose. That was also a shift for me. Then along came Anne.*

Once Paulo began to see relationships as an opportunity for joy, connection and sharing, he began to journal about the kind of woman he wished to meet. Soon Anne came into his life. Paulo and Anne are together to this day and share a special relationship as best friends and life partners.

> *We made a covenant to grow old together. We chose to break from tradition and to live our lives more by love and less by contract.*

Paulo found additional ways to make space for his I-F. One day, while noticing two women talking animatedly over pictures of one woman's cat, he thought "look at that love."

> *I said to Anne that night, "Why haven't we ever got a cat or a dog? Why haven't we allowed this before?"*

A few days later they got "Lady", a mischievous and fun-loving tabby cat from the local SPCA.

> *I look at how besotted we've become over our cat and then I think to myself "that's an energy that you previously denied to yourself."*

For the first time Paulo began to take more interest in his home environment.

> *I had already begun to integrate the feminine but it occurred to me I also had to allow it into my surroundings. For the first time I started to take an interest in what my home looked like, what my couches were going to be covered in and what my table looked like. Prior to that, it would be something I'd phone my sisters for. It's like I'd outsourced my feminine energy.*

Paulo also undertook what would have been unthinkable in his youth: he painted his first picture. "I was so proud of it!" he recalls.

How balance changed his life

> *It is hard to express the depth of the shift that has taken place. The Paulo after the Reiki experience is a more balanced, more grounded... a better person. The one that existed before was so task-driven.*
>
> *It is still a strong theme in my life, but I've learned about the other side – the nurturing energy, the patient energy,*

> *the creative energy. Since I've made peace with that I'm no longer so interested in things that just appeal to my brain. Thinking, for me, is the male, logical way of doing things. "If you do this and this and this, that will be the outcome." There is no room for the emotional. There is no room for any of the feel-good stuff. If you don't have that balance, you are missing out on life.*
>
> *There was a time when a sunset didn't move me at all. It was just an opportunity to take a nice picture to show someone. But it didn't mean anything. Whereas now, the beauty of a sunset can make me cry.*
>
> *My life is also simpler. I started developing a stronger sense of 'enough' which is a clear shift away from the need for material validation, something so important to me in the past.*

Next, Paulo highlights a significant insight about how balance has changed his life.

> *One of the prices I paid in having that black-and-white mentality is that in a lot of cases it puts the onus for life and success and responsibility purely 100% on you.*
>
> *It's as if the only person who can shape your destiny is you. And I've now learned that this is not entirely true. I think that is half the picture. You certainly initiate it and get it going but then life and people will come and collude with you and it'll happen if you let it. Whereas when you were in black-and-white mode, everything was up to you. Once I began to tap the other side of the energy I started to allow things to happen that I wouldn't ordinarily have and they would turn out really well for me. And I would think "wow, I would never have gone there on my own."*

Another shift has been in his management style.

> *I did this change with people too. My management style before allowed no room for others – there was "the Paulo way of doing it" and that was the way. It makes sense for business and all that. But it certainly didn't allow any space for others. The people weren't inspired, nor did their creativity come out. This is denying yourself the value of being able to have access to that wonderful creativity that's in other people because you're only seeing in black and white.*

His approach to business changed significantly.

> *I find that a lot of academic, thinking stuff fits on the side of logic and what I call male energy. I'm not saying only men think. I'm saying "thinking" so whether it's a man or a woman doing it, it's the same thing.*
>
> *I've done a few business turnarounds. I look at the business and discover there's a mindset. I realize "You [the company's leadership] are being far too logical about all of this." Then I smile to myself and think "and what's missing is that other energy. That's why you're getting into trouble here."*
>
> *They can make a very good argument for what they are doing and they bring all their research and it all makes logical sense. But it doesn't work! Nine times out of ten that is what's missing: that other energy is not brought into play.*

I asked Paulo what is the impact of excessive I-M in these situations.

> *I think male energy can often stifle creativity and natural ability. It becomes too dominant and doesn't allow for anything but itself. I'm not just criticizing male energy; I recognize its value. But when it gets like this, it stifles our true potential. It doesn't know that there's more.*

Paulo tells the story of what happened in a business venture when he and Anne returned to South Africa after having lived in the UK for five years.

> *I returned home to take ownership of the franchise business I had previously started and sold to my business partner. By now the business was worth millions. Sadly, soon after this, I got into a dispute with my partner. On paper, and by all accounts, I was on the right side of the dispute. Eventually we got to a point where he played a devious legal card, ironically a trick I had taught him before in my black-and-white days. It was the type of trick that could be justified by that calculated male energy mode – "winning at all costs." I was furious.*
>
> *On the Friday night I went to the head of the litigation department of one of the top law firms in the country. After consultation with a little army of legal experts we were going to take legal action and serve an interdict against him on Monday morning.*
>
> *My attorney said to me "This is no time for emotion. It's clinical. We go in, do what's needed regardless of the dire consequences for your partner." When I left the offices I was shaking. As I sat that night thinking about this, I got a clear image of me, like Troy, going to war with a formidable army. I knew it would obliterate my partner because he was trying to take advantage of me and I had the law firmly on my side.*

Paulo had no doubt that suing his partner, a close family relative, would have ruined him and led to all his material property being seized.

> *But at 3 am on Sunday morning, while agonizing over this, I asked myself "Is this really the road I want to go down? Do I really want to go back to being the Paulo of the past?"*

Paulo contemplated a future with a family rift and all the drama and pain associated with it.

> *I believe what happened was: my female energy got a chance. Whereas the day before, there was no female energy in the equation. I had the national authority on intellectual property there. I knew "I'm going to war and my God, do I have an army." Then the next day the female energy had a turn, and I woke up on Sunday morning, and had an open discussion with Anne. We took things in a different direction. We decided not to prosecute. We gave the business back without any terms or conditions and got out.*
>
> *Prior to this shift I would have gone ahead with it. I knew I would win, but I chose a different outcome. My decision-making process has definitely changed.*

The dance

How does Paulo relate to his I-F and I-M now that he is a lot more balanced?

> *You are sort of indifferent to either one, so you access it as and when, and it accesses you as and when.*
>
> *When you said "It's a dance" I got it. But it's a dance with no leading partner. Because the leading partner dance is the one my Dad taught me where the male leads. But this is a dance with no leading partner. It's a dance that goes where it feels and thinks... it just happens.*

When decisions need to be made Paulo now consults both sides of himself.

> *I find myself consciously saying "have I only looked at this situation from a logical point of view or have I also looked at it from a heart point of view?" A lot of times it will change what I'm thinking. When I have an idea and*

> *I apply that, I end up changing it in either direction. I've found that very helpful.*
>
> *I've found that conflict has reduced quite a bit, especially in work situations. I'm using a more accommodating approach. It's that dance taking place.*

How did Paulo make this shift work for him?

> *In the beginning the male energy was crossing every "t" and dotting every "i", "let's read this thing backwards just to make sure, just in case." Whereas before the masculine energy felt it needed to make every decision and then go out and take responsibility for its decision and implement it and make it work, it now says "I don't have to make every decision." There are a lot of decisions in the past that I would have taken and scrutinized into the ground.*
>
> *The energy now says: just back off a little bit and allow this decision to be made. Instead of fighting with the decision, rather use your ability and your strength to look at it and say "I would never have looked at it like that but now that I consider that, I think I can make it work. I think I can take my energy and power and rather than focusing it primarily on the decision that must be made - I can throw it* behind *the decision that's being made."*

This was a powerful insight that reflects a quintessential aspect of the relationship between I-M and I-F: rather than getting in the way, I-M can figure out how best to support I-F in terms of what it wants and where it wants to go. This is the flow of inner compass with aligned action.

Finally, I asked Paulo to say more about "the dance."

> *Through your masculine and feminine energies, you begin to do a dance with life. This means that there will be times when life will take you. You might think you*

need to go this way but life will take you that way. It won't tell you but you'll feel it. It will just take you there and you won't question it because you believe in it.

As a result, going in that direction, which you would never have gone on your own, opens up a lot of doors and opportunities. I feel very strongly that that is where the greatest value has been added to my life. I suddenly began to realize this thing called life – I don't have to do on my own. Actually I'm not here to do it on my own, I'm here to be part of it. And when you begin to have that mindset you look at a lot of things differently.

All of a sudden, environmental conservation and things like that make sense, whereas before it didn't really make sense. It was more of a hindrance because your thinking was very goal-focused. I can understand where you create problems with unintended consequences but you did it because you were thinking in black and white and all of a sudden color problems came along.

You just have to agree to dance with the energies and say, "OK, I hear you. I see you. You're there. There's female energy. There's a male energy. Let me understand you, like I would with any human being. If I want to develop a relationship with you, I must get to know you better." So to me that's all you have to do. And then it will dance with you. Whether you want to dance with it or not, it will dance with you if you acknowledge it. Because if you acknowledge it you allow it to be and then it can impact you.

One must simply be more conscious.

How does Paulo know which side of himself to engage in any moment?

The situation tells me "We need male energy here and we need female energy there. We need a combination here."

Every situation has a "dosage" requirement. That's what's happening now. Instead of me just giving it a good old dose of male energy I find I'm using another approach.

Up until I was aware of this difference, I thought I was very powerful. Boy oh boy, did I think I was powerful! Once that shift happened, I realized, your power was a fraction of what it could be. It's at so many levels that I experienced this, where I realized there's huge power in having the balance.

With inner balance power is greatly enhanced as it becomes so much more than just one person's will in action. Being inclusive unleashes the creative power of others, creating better solutions. This is "power with" others. In many ways I think my male energy is being expressed far more powerfully now and its real potential is being expressed because I am no longer burdening it with too much.

In a way I've set it free and it can do what it does when it needs to. So it doesn't have this burden of authority and responsibility and "I've got to make every decision" and it's got to pass this black-and-white-male-thinking test.

I've got to a point where I say "Ok that's where it wants to take me. My brain is probably going to come up with 50 reasons why I shouldn't do this, but you know what, I'm going to go with it, look at it and satisfy myself through my brain that I can make this work."

Paulo's story shows that anyone can become balanced once the decision is made to do so – even a previously hardened businessman with a tough-guy image.

Paulo's story illustrates that the benefits of balance are enormous. He feels that he has become a better person thanks to his inner balance. He is happier within himself. His relationships have improved. There is color and richness in his life. There is passion and purpose. He has learned the subtle art of letting go and being guided by life itself rather than struggling to control it. As a business consultant and speaker, Paulo is more powerful than ever before. He still uses his sharp mind to benefit businesses but now he brings heart into the equation. That changes *everything*.

CHAPTER 10

How Balanced Are We as Individuals?

As an individual it is possible to have an excess of either I-M or I-F. It is also possible to have excesses of each at different times.

During the day or at different places and with different people we might be inclined one way but at night, weekends or in other situations it might be the opposite. There are many possible permutations and combinations.

Excessive I-M

What are some everyday signs of excessive I-M unbalanced by I-F?

- Working excessively and struggling with work-life balance
- Being unable to relax and unwind even while on vacation
- Working excessively as "a badge of honor"
- Staying in an uninspiring job
- Being cerebral; living "from the head up"
- A tendency to be controlling and difficulty "letting go"
- Feeling the lack of a sense of purpose in life
- A tendency to get stuck in details, unable to see the big picture
- Being unable to connect to inner guidance and inspiration
- Being overly competitive

In each, I-M is in overdrive. When I was in corporate ladder climbing mode during my twenties, I could relate to every one of them.

Penelope, the entrepreneur who farms in Malawi, speaks of her struggle to balance work with rest and rejuvenation:

> *I am capable of just hammering and hammering and hammering at my work until I keel over. We're not taught in a place like the UK to give ourselves a break.*
>
> *I'm only just learning to meditate and breathe. Yet, I still self-sabotage because I don't do it. I know it's so beneficial yet I don't get to do it. Why? It's something I'm battling to make the time for, yet I know it's so beneficial.*

It is up to us to build it into our lives. Life does not hand "downtime" to us. We must create it in our reality by first creating it within ourselves, in our very being.

As long as one side of us is calling the shots, nothing changes. I discovered that changing my lifestyle and habits required an internal shift and a reshuffling of my priorities. This is not a mental exercise like simply choosing this over that. It requires an entire paradigm shift.

Only by allowing and welcoming my I-F to rise *and be as important as my I-M* could I live from that space and create the balance I yearned for.

Penelope's example illustrates what happens when the I-F – our ability to surrender, yield, let go, be passive – is not sufficiently *enlivened*.

Many fear surrendering or yielding, confusing these for being weak. In its healthy form it is surrendering to your higher self, inner knowing, heart and the beauty around you.

While living in Berkeley, California (renowned for its progressive and alternative mindset) I laughed at a car bumper sticker that read: "Don't just do something. Sit there!" This is the challenge for most people with busy lives.

In an interview with Lisa Garr on *The Aware Show* on Hay House Radio (86), writer, director and producer Barnet Bain expressed a strong desire to change his approach to life and film-making.

Barnet Bain produces Hollywood movies including the Academy Award-winning film, *What Dreams May Come* and *The Celestine Prophecy*. He says:

> *I am tired of coming from a place of being in a relationship with the world that requires you to be constantly coming only with will and action. There is an emptiness to that. So I didn't want to come at the world with just will and action. "Just do it, just do it," that monkey mentality.*
>
> *I wanted to balance it with being.*
>
> *There are trees outside my house. They are not "just doing it." There is an ocean out there. It is not filled with will and action. There is certainly a lot of action but there's also a lot of just being. I wanted to explore the relationship of will and action along with connecting and imagining and feeling, "just being" states.*
>
> *For me this is counter-logical. The logical mind says there's a way to get movies made. You have to do, do, do, action steps. I've done enough action steps in my life but I'm willing and prepared to do something in the unknown now and just be vulnerable and say "I may fail at this."*
>
> *It would be a real affront to my ego, I may fail at this in a very public way. I may, and I'm willing to because I want to explore what is it to say to the world, to God: "I trust and I want to live in that trust and it's not entirely up to me to do and push and push and push, and I'm going to put out something that I think is beautiful."*

Bain is expressing a yearning for balance, specifically to enliven his I-F as an integral part of his approach to work and life.

Tired of being stuck in logic, will and action as the only ways to get things done, he wants to create something of beauty from a co-creative space of trust and being in the flow.

Excessive I-F

It is also possible to develop excessive I-F, either as an entire way of being or just in specific areas of life.

Here are some everyday examples:

- Depleting yourself in the course of nurturing others
- Giving your power away just to stay in a relationship
- Habitually putting yourself last
- Being timid and shy
- Having great ideas but not taking action to make them happen
- Being a "Jack-or-Jill-of-all-trades" but a master of none
- Being unable to get your career or other projects going
- Being run by emotions
- Being emotionally manipulative
- Using substances to attempt to feel good

Women are known to struggle with the first two bullet points because society presents the image of "a good mother" or "a good wife" as someone who prioritizes others' needs over their own. But this can be taken too far and rather than being "noble" it can simply be a case of self-abandonment.

Erin, a 50-year old fitness instructor and former stuntwoman, illustrates the journey of a woman who learned to take cognizance of her own needs and eventually put them above a relationship that was hurting her.

> *As a lively, happy soul, Erin is easily the life of any party. Today Erin is happily married to her second husband and the mother of two teenage daughters. But life wasn't always this good.*
>
> *Erin's first marriage was to an abusive man. She describes this part of her life as a nightmare.*
>
> *"He was controlling and insecure, always putting me down. As a result, my self-esteem was decimated."*

> *For a time, they lived in Greece where they had no car. Erin managed to earn a small but sufficient income as a fitness instructor at a local gym.*
>
> *Since they lived on a mountain pass, her mode of transport was a bicycle. To spite her, Erin's husband often dismantled the bicycle just before she needed to leave for work. She soon learned to reassemble the bicycle in double-quick time – and get to work without being late.*
>
> *Not wanting to see the relationship for what it was, Erin kept trying to make it work. After two years together she realized it was pointless. After returning home she decided to leave him. That was not easy but she did what she had to do: put herself first.*

Erin's story is that of a woman who in many ways has a strong and healthy connection to her I-M, but in one area – relationships – she struggled initially with the signs of excessive I-F.

As with excessive I-M, situations involving excessive I-F can only be changed from the inside. Many people realize this only when they hit a crisis that forces them to consider their own needs. The shift requires getting in touch with their I-M, that part that says, "Wait a minute. What about me? What about my needs?"

If life is a balance between "taking care of others' needs" and "taking care of my needs," our foundation must be the latter. Without this we risk running on empty, attempting to keep giving from an empty cup.

We can only effectively be of service to others when we ourselves are sufficiently energized and our needs have been taken care of. For this to happen we must have sufficient I-M to balance the desire to put the needs of others first.

The journey from excessive to balanced energy

Even in excessive polarized energy there is still the hint of something positive.

In excessive I-F, the tendency to nurture at one's own expense still contains the ability to nurture. In excessive I-M, the tendency to be a workaholic still contains the ability to apply oneself and be outcome-oriented.

That relationship, it turns out, is key to understanding the path to balance.

Each mature quality has an immature version

In chapter 2 we explored a myriad of I-F and I-M qualities (Table 1). You may have noticed those are all positive, desirable qualities. For example, the I-F ability to nurture and the I-M ability to use logical reasoning. These are considered mature qualities.

However, *every one of these qualities (in Table 1) has an immature equivalent.*

An easy test for knowing whether a certain behavior is mature or not is whether it is preceded by the words "is able to" vs. "can only." If you are *able to* nurture others, that's a mature quality. If you *can only* nurture others and don't know when to stop to take care of yourself, that is the immature equivalent of nurturing.

"Immature I-M" is synonymous with "unbalanced I-M", "excessive masculine" and "hypermasculine." The same relationship applies to the I-F equivalents.

As we evolve we grow into the mature

Our collective purpose is to grow from the immature to the mature version of all I-M and I-F energies. Like a magnificent tree that begins as a tiny sapling, we begin with the immature but our purpose is to grow into our full potential.

For some the growth from immature to mature in a particular area happens very fast. For others, it could take an entire lifetime – or even many lifetimes.

In *Destiny of Souls*, Michael Newton (87), a clinical hypnotherapist discovered that a client took 800 years to learn forgiveness (over several lifetimes). The difference lies in the degree of conscious awareness and orientation to life itself. When life is lived from an "unconscious" perspective in reactive mode, change can take years. When lived from an attitude of conscious awareness and openness it can take months, weeks or a split second to make a desirable shift. It is a mind-shift accompanied by the willingness to shift in habit.

The difference between immature and mature qualities is shown in Table 2 (I-F qualities) and Table 3 (I-M qualities).

Table 2: Immature to mature I-F qualities

Immature I-F	Mature I-F
Lack of self-awareness	Self-awareness
Lack of a sense of purpose	In touch with your purpose
Nurturing at one's own expense	Ability to nurture
Relationships at all costs	Ability to be in a relationship
Unassertive, popularity-contest management style	People-oriented and coaching management style
Fun at all costs	Ability to have fun
Escapism and addictions as an attempt to feel happiness	Ability to cultivate happiness as a state of being
Mulling over issues to the point of depression	Ability to transform your inner environment (thoughts and feelings)
Being "all over the place", jumping from this to that, e.g. in a conversation	Being able to collate the pieces and see the big picture
Use of emotional manipulation to achieve desired outcomes	Power to attract desired outcomes from within (Law of Attraction)
Unassertive leadership and a need to be liked	Quiet leadership or Transformational leadership

Table 3: Immature to mature I-M qualities

Immature I-M	Mature I-M
Unhealthy self-expression	Healthy self-expression
Unable to bring projects to fruition	Able to bring projects to fruition
Power at all costs/Power over	Supportive and empowering behavior toward self and others
Autocratic and micromanaging	Mentoring and task-orientation
Achievement at all costs	Enjoying achievement when it happens
Workaholic	Deriving satisfaction from work
Aggressive, bullying communication	Assertive, clear communication
Narrow, reductionist thinking	Methodical, structured thinking
Overly competitive/ winning is everything	Healthy competition/focus on self-improvement
Autocratic leadership	Transactional leadership

To illustrate, here is the story of Joanna, whose journey to balance took her from being a successful but driven businesswoman to stepping back due to challenging life circumstances, and then discovering her true passion and creating a business out of that.

From workaholic to healing entrepreneur: Joanna's story

Joanna is a dynamic woman in her early fifties. Having being raised by parents who were self-employed, she expected to be financially independent from an early age. By the age of 35 Joanna was running three companies with 56 employees. She ran a dairy farm, a yoghurt factory and she owned and ran a mail-order confectionary and gift franchises which had 7 franchisees. She married and had two sons and maintained the businesses while raising a family.

At this point Joanna had relied a lot on her masculine energy to get things done.

Then things took a turn. A prolonged court case usurped much of Joanna's time and energy, resulting in burnout and thyroid problems. She realized in retrospect she had driven herself too hard.

A year later her marriage broke up.

Joanna began to question the meaning of her life. This started her on a spiritual quest. She decided to sell her businesses, simplify her life and reduce her responsibilities. She needed to recover her energy and figure out what to do next.

To attain this, she went from being an employer to an employee, working in the corporate world for the next four years. Joanna and her children moved back to the suburbs and soon thereafter, her parents moved in with them because they were physically and mentally ailing.

Joanna began to take care of her parents. Her father was becoming paralyzed with Gillian Barr syndrome and her mother developed Alzheimer's disease. Looking after her mother was "like having a two-year old back in the house". Joanna began to do Reiki on her parents, with good results. As a result of her caretaking role she learned to be more compassionate and patient.

Joanna reinvented herself from being a successful business entrepreneur operating predominantly from her masculine energy. Life circumstances gave her new opportunities to tune into her feminine energy in different ways. As a result, she experienced a shift. She became drawn to energy healing as a vocation.

Due to debts owed on the farm, despite selling her businesses, her money soon ran out. Remarkably, Joanna was not phased.

She is now building a new career as an intuitive and energy healer. Joanna trusts her ability to create financial abundance as she did in the past, but it is no longer all up to her. She trusts in a higher power, feels a greater sense of purpose and believes the universe will support her in achieving it.

Joanna exudes a beautiful balance of masculine and feminine energies. Since her big shift, she says, "my happiness levels have soared".

Joanna's story shows that sometimes life nudges us in the direction of balance even if we don't think we're ready for it. What may be appear to be a disaster can be a turning point that brings an opportunity to create more balance within ourselves and live a more purpose-driven life.

The more mature our qualities, the more balanced we are

The degree of inner balance and the maturity of our attributes go hand-in-hand.

The reason for this is: to get to the mature quality of any attribute we need to cultivate an element of "opposite sex energy." Balance is *required* for maturity of any attribute.

The difference between "is able to use logical reasoning" and "can only think with logical reasoning" is the presence of absence of I-F, respectively.

In this example, cultivating more I-F enables us to use logical reasoning when needed, but have other options available. This is how we graduate from "can only" to "is able to."

This is explored visually in the Journey-to-Balance Model in chapter 12. For now, it is helpful to know that inner balance is possible when the mature versions of qualities have been cultivated.

The more balanced a person is, the more mature their qualities are, and vice versa.

Ego vs. Self

The difference between mature and immature qualities is the degree to which ego is present. Ego is defined as the "little self", the part of us concerned with personal survival, security, power and image. The difference between being assertive vs being a bully is the degree to which ego is running the show.

The more balanced and mature we become the more we are operating from Self (our spiritual self or higher self). The less balanced we are, the more we are operating from ego.

As individuals we must navigate through different expressions of imbalance and grow into balance and maturity. To get to the better angels of our nature we must participate in the quintessential human journey of transcending the ego.

CHAPTER 11

What Does Balance Really Mean?

"Does it mean I have to wear a skirt?" a man asks.

"Will this make me androgynous?"

"Will they think I'm gay?"

These questions come up from time to time. The question underlying these is: what does it mean (and not mean) to be balanced?

Knowing the difference makes all the difference. That's what makes it possible to cultivate inner balance with comfort and ease.

What balance means

1. Enlivening both sides so that you can draw upon them as needed

This is the quintessence of balance: being able to draw upon and express any part of your I-M and I-F energies as needed in the moment. This means being able to dial them up or down as needed, so that you can handle situations most effectively. This is the same concept as "gender fluidity."

Life brings a multitude of experiences, opportunities and challenges requiring us to draw from our I-M and I-F energies.

Cultivating balance makes you well-rounded yet it doesn't mean having to lose focus on your particular interests and passions. It brings life to the next level.

As a corporate coach, I navigate the intersecting world of business and human potential. Client sessions may call for a mix of deep listening, intuitive responses, logical thinking, compassion, tough love and an understanding of the business and its strategy. Being fully present to serve my clients requires a whole range of inputs.

One coaching client had tears in his eyes while explaining that he felt he had missed his calling to become a pilot. Instead, here he was, an IT professional, good at his job but frustrated with life. His relationship with colleagues and with a significant client was strained. It didn't help that he had a temper.

Yet, within a few weeks, he had shifted into a positive, focused professional. His relationships improved and he started becoming more self-referring rather than easily affected by others. After cutting back on his drinking and returning to daily exercise at the gym, he was almost a different man when I saw him weeks later. Working with him required drawing from a wide range of my resources. If I had been in tune with *either* my feminine side *or* my masculine side, I would not have reached him effectively.

Drawing upon both sides: Andrew's story

Andrew is an industrial engineer who helps companies save money by optimizing their inventory. In this line of work Andrew needs to deal with a great deal of complexity and "moving parts." This involves the company, its supply chain and the products that end up as inventory.

Andrew's mental flexibility and his ability to see the big picture, both I-F qualities, stand him in good stead to get an overall understanding of each client and what their needs are.

The technical side of his work requires sharp focus, excellent analytical skills and high degree of precision – all I-M qualities – all of which he is exceptionally good at.

Many industrial engineers have the technical skills to do this work. Andrew takes it a step further by weaving his feminine energies into the equation. The combination of his I-M and I-F energies makes him exceptional. He has a tremendous ability to connect with clients. This is enabled by his exceptional ability to listen. This I-F capability brings his technical work to new levels precisely because of tuning in to client needs and addressing them specifically.

When providing training all across the globe, delegates often marvel at how interesting and accessible he makes the material no matter their prior level of experience.

How did Andrew get to this place? He acknowledges that as a young man he had a lot of I-M. He was analytical, astute and focused. At the age of seventeen, a career counsellor advised him to follow a career in engineering or science – and stay away from people-oriented careers!

Yet as a young man he realized that he wanted to become more balanced. He started cultivating his feminine side.

He did this in various ways. During his twenties he became a vegetarian, a daily meditator and even a meditation teacher. This enlivened his inner world and his relationship with himself. He developed a healthy lifestyle based on alternative health principles. This brought awareness, relaxation, rhythm and health.

During his thirties he became a hands-on father. He actively shared in child raising and in all domestic responsibilities. He learned to "relax into" daily activities such as cooking or washing the dishes, without hurrying it along. These were simply activities one could choose to enjoy by being fully present.

Andrew started his own business in part so that he could work from home and be an active part of family life. Together with his wife he started a school where children could learn meditation and receive a holistic education.

Now in his Sixties, Andrew is a well-rounded and exceptional human being. He is precise and analytical when needed, yet is warm-hearted, open-minded, patient, fun-loving, gentle and compassionate. Getting to *this place was a conscious journey and was well worth it. The outcomes speak for themselves.*

2. Maintaining your interests but pursuing them from a balanced perspective

Being balanced does not render us all the same. It means pursuing our own distinct and unique interests *from a place of balance.*

Andrew's story illustrates this remarkably well: he remained true to his technical interests but over time approached his work differently. As he undertook the journey toward wholeness by gradually integrating many elements of his I-F, he brought a whole new "energy" to his work. By including intuition and the big picture, and applying wonderful people skills he brought his professional offering to a new level.

As unique expressions of Source, we all have our own personality, talents and interests. Yet, at our deepest level, just like Source, we are balanced. Coming from a place of balance makes our contributions more effective, beneficial and sustainable. This brings our contributions to a new level.

By contrast, whatever is created from a place of imbalance is at best only partially beneficial.

Here are examples of what it could look like to stick to our interests, but pursue them from a space of balance:

- Sue, an automotive engineer, excels in the technical aspects of her work (I-M). Being balanced, she also sees the big picture. She is aware of the future potential impact of millions of these cars on the environment (I-F). Her technical expertise is combined with her care for the environment to design a green technology car.
- Doug, a real estate agent, enjoys and connects with people (I-F) yet is able to keep healthy boundaries, structure his time and manage the legal and administrative details effectively (I-M). This combination optimizes his success. Any part left out would thwart his success.
- John, a cell phone engineer, designs a technologically sound device (I-M). Being a balanced person he cares for the wellbeing

of people (I-F). He therefore builds into the design ways to mitigate the negative effects of EMFs, electromagnetic pollution that emanates from electronic devices. He tests different materials and creates a phone that is technologically sound *and* healthy for people. This is far greater than the technology alone.

- Sharon, a psychologist, is caring and compassionate (I-F). She also maintains healthy boundaries with clients, keeps up with research and is comfortable charging clients adequately for her services (I-M). In addition, Sharon is open to alternative therapies (I-F). This adds a new dimension to her work. This combination of elements enables her to help people effectively while being financially sustainable.

As these examples show, being balanced does not require us to pursue areas not of interest. Sue and John, both in traditional male jobs, don't have to take up sewing in an attempt to be balanced if sewing is not of interest. Doug and Sharon, both in traditional female jobs, don't have to become car enthusiasts to be balanced. Each can be true to themselves.

New skills and areas of knowledge may need to be added but these still pertain to the chosen field of work and can only add to its effectiveness.

On a large scale this would create a world of individuals pursuing work that is specifically of interest to them, and yet bringing a balanced and creative perspective to their work.

3. Still you, but a more effective version

For anyone entertaining fear about balance it is now clear: being balanced is being *you* – only a more effective version.

At its most basic level balance is "acting in alignment with your inner compass."

Being connected with your inner compass (I-F), you can be true to yourself. When you're tired, you rest. When you've had enough, you stop. When it comes to your ideal work, you are able to discover what it is.

With your masculine side, the engine (I-M), in place, you are poised to take action in alignment with your dreams and goals.

Being in touch with both aspects affords you the best possible chance of a purposeful life with work that combines effectiveness, functionality, sustainability, care, beauty and fun.

A more effective Erin

You may recall Erin, the 50-year old fitness instructor and former stuntwoman from before. Here is the rest of her story which illustrates that through balance, we become more, not less, of who we are.

> *For the sheer fun of it, Erin runs a popular boogie-boarding group for women. The group meets weekly throughout the year and charges no fees. It attracts a community of fifty to sixty women of all ages.*

After leaving an abusive partner, as described before, Erin she began a new life.

> *One thing Erin could always rely on was her physical strength and stamina. This got her thinking "What about stunt work?"*

> *On the first day doing stunt work she met the man who was to become her second husband, a stuntman himself. For many years Erin did stunt work for movies and advertisements. She laughs uproariously about the day she had to do the same bungee jump five times over because of various failures to film the scene properly.*

> *Erin carried on with stunt work after her daughters were born but eventually slowed down and discontinued due to the toll it took on her body. She then switched back to fitness instruction.*

> *Erin and her husband are the greatest of friends. He often spends up to a month away on stunt work projects. While he's away she just gets on with things. When he gets back she is thrilled. Either way, she remains happy.*

This in itself shows a mature degree of inner balance: the fact that Erin is happy when she's alone and happy with her husband's companionship. While she has a deeply loving relationship him, she is not dependent on him for her happiness. Being self-contained, she spends time alone easily.

> *Erin is a loving, caring mother to her two teenage daughters, a role she very much enjoys. At the same time, she honors her need for freedom and fun outside her role as a parent. Erin confided: "I'm not one of those mothers who cannot separate themselves from their children. I adore being a mother, but it's one aspect of who I am."*

> *She usually cannot wait to get back into the waves with the other boogie board riders. Erin usually heads for the backline where the real surfers hang out. She surfs a wave as well as any.*

> *Erin feels that her next step in her personal growth involves developing her spiritual and intuitive faculties, opening up further aspects of her I-F.*

Erin's journey to balance is interesting. She has always been in touch with many aspects of her I-M: her sense of freedom, independence and physical strength. Yet in her first marriage she experienced "relationship at all costs" for a period of time. To move beyond this, she needed the support of her I-M to say in effect: "Wait a minute. What about me?" This part of her came through and enabled her to create a wonderful new life.

While Erin has remained connected to her adventurous and free-spirited ways, life began to present new opportunities to connect with her I-F – first as a loving wife and then as a mother. This opened her to new levels of love and nurturing. Even so, Erin did not experience life as a pendulum between her I-F and I-M but as two aspects of her that are co-present. Even while become more loving and nurturing, she never lost her independent and free-spirited ways. Through balance Erin has become more of who she is. Her light shines more brightly than at any other time in her life.

What balance does *not* mean

1. Having to dress or behave like the opposite sex

Sometimes I hear men say jokingly: "Does this mean I have to wear dresses?" No, you don't.

As my own journey taught me, integrating I-F has little to do with wearing dresses, make-up and high heels. It is a set of psycho-spiritual capabilities that are enlivened within, and available to be expressed as needed.

What about women?

A British survey of 2,000 working women (88) shows that 25% of women believe it is necessary to dress in a more masculine way – wearing dark trouser suits for example, in order to be treated seriously at work. This is understandable since masculine qualities are more highly valued in many work settings.

Rather than criticizing women for exercising this choice, as is often the case, it could simply be recognized as a legitimate phase in their journey to balance. Embracing their I-M does not necessitate wearing androgynous clothes but it could be part of the journey. It may be possible that a woman who feels established in her state of balance may revert back to more feminine attire. Or she may prefer androgynous attire. This is entirely a matter of free will.

A further 25% of corporate women wear less make up, partly to dispel the idea that women "should look pretty." In a world that still operates with gender stereotypes, this reasoning is understandable.

Men and women ought to be free to dress in whatever way is comfortable.

Some men dress conservatively: blue, black and beige. Others prefer more color and flair.

Some women dress more androgynously to make a statement. Some dress with a focus on style and comfort. Others prefer very feminine attire with more of a focus on looks.

When it comes to balance, what counts is not what we wear: it is what's on the inside. What is your preferred style of dress?

2. *Having your sexual preference in question*

This issue may crop up among some heterosexuals: a fear that inner balance means having to behave like the opposite sex, thus coming across "gay" or "butch."

Outward behavior, mannerisms, voice and ways of speaking are not changed by becoming balanced. These are part of who you are. If you identify as a male, then as a balanced person you will still come across as a male. The same applies to females.

Each person interviewed for this book exuded a fascinating combination of I-M and I-F energies regardless of being in a male or a female body. This introduces an intriguing "x-factor" which is very attractive.

3. *Being stuck in the middle of the road*

Being balanced is *not* being stuck in the grey middle of the road at the mid-point between the I-M and I-F poles. That would be a misunderstanding of balance.

Inner balance is a dynamic and fluctuating state of being that encompasses both sides.

Andrew's story demonstrates that balance means operating from anywhere in the spectrum between masculine to feminine.

When Andrew focuses on technicalities, this is his I-M. A moment later, someone may need his attention and he quickly switches to an open, attentive mode with a high quality of listening. This is his I-F.

While engaging with a client he might switch from the big picture view (I-F) to the detailed view (I-M) many times in a few seconds. That is like going from the extreme left side of the road to the extreme right side of the road in a few seconds. There is nothing "grey" or "middle of the road" about that.

Being balanced means you can occupy *any point* in the road.

The "average placement" might be somewhere near the middle but that is the nature of a bell curve: depending on its symmetry, the average is in the middle. Each situation and event could occur anywhere on the extreme left or right, or anywhere in-between. That is nothing but pure freedom.

4. That you cannot at times indulge in one side

You can indulge in one side for a time and still be balanced.

The *Law of Balance* as I see it says: you can immerse yourself for a time in either masculine or feminine energy – and that this creates growth and learning. It can also be a lot of fun. If you want to thrive however, you must return to center.

One example is sex. This is where sexual differences come into play and where it can be fun to accentuate the differences and enjoy the chemistry. The difference is, it's a game and it is not confused with a permanent sense of identity.

Here's what Mark, an author and coach, says:

> *I find pleasure in the sexual match of male and female energy. Sarah [his partner] is very balanced, and in some areas of life she is more masculine than me. But still there is a play of male-female energy. It's an understanding that it's totally equal but there is difference. There's a flirting there. It's almost a dance you're playing with the other person.*
>
> *It doesn't define who you are but it's something to play with while having sex.*
>
> *I've realized why I wasn't getting as much sex before. I hadn't figured that you can play the roles lightly and that is a good thing. You can play the powerful man, as*

long as you realize it's a game. It's about the energy. Once you realize it's a dance - like where he throws her on the table – that's fire. For a woman it can be wonderful!

Sometimes it would be nice to have a reversal, where the woman takes the lead. Many men find it a burden after a while because it's always the act and the performance and initiating. Women are experiencing their wild side and that's great. A woman's embodied, sensual power can be amazing to explore. It's also a dance.

Part of life is enjoying your body and the experiences it gives you.

Another example is stay-at-home mothers and fathers. Staying at home to raise children is an immersion in the feminine.

This role may continue for some time and this is OK.

The same goes for sole breadwinners. There may be times when it makes more sense to allow yourself and your partner to function differently for a period of time. This is part of the exploration and journey of life and it brings its own learnings and benefits.

Indulging in one side of yourself is fine as long as it doesn't become the source of your identity.

What if I cannot fully balance?

Don't worry. Just do your best. It is not a competition. Progress is measured only against your former self.

You have already progressed since the start of this book. By now you have gained a more in-depth understanding of what it really means to balance.

CHAPTER 12

The Journey-to-Balance Model

Now that you know what balance is all about you can begin to assess your own state of balance. This is where the juice is!

For this purpose, I introduce the *Journey-to-Balance Model,* which I will call "the model" from here on.

This is a unique model that came to me intuitively. I wanted to arrive at a holistic model that encompasses the polarities of masculine-feminine and different levels of maturity. One day it came to me as a complete picture.

The model presents a bird's eye view that enables you to determine your current state of balance and know how to create more balance where needed.

The Model

It is divided into four quadrants: Immature I-F, Mature I-F, Immature I-M and Mature I-M.

Please note the term "immature" is not intended as a value statement but merely as a way of discerning between the highly desirable mature state of I-F or I-M and the developing state that is its precursor. If you should happen to discover an element of yourself that falls into the "immature" zone, it does not make you an immature person: it just means that there is a part of you that is operating in its "developing stage". We all have aspects like that.

Each quadrant has a specific "essence" and is distinct from the others. The left half of the model represents I-F and the right half, I-M. The bottom half represents the immature half, where unbalanced I-M and I-F play out. The top half is the mature half to which we all aspire, where balanced energy plays out.

The model focuses on 10 day-to-day aspects of life, including the way we relate to ourselves and others, and the way we approach happiness, power and leadership. It teases each of these out into the four quadrants with clear relationships between them.

The 10 areas represent our relationship or approach to:

1. Oneself
2. Others
3. Knowing
4. Thinking
5. Happiness
6. Conflict Resolution
7. People Management
8. Time Management
9. Power
10. Leadership

The Journey-to-Balance Model is shown in Figure 1.

Figure 1: Journey-to-Balance Model

Mature

Relationship to:

1 Oneself	Self-awareness/Self-esteem/Self-love/Sense of purpose	Healthy, self-supporting actions/Able to bring things to fruition
2 Others	Empathic, caring relationships from a strong sense of self	Partner as equal/Supportive, empowering, loving behavior
3 Knowing	Intuition/Body/Holistic, integrated awareness	Logic/Detailed knowledge of the parts
4 Thinking	Big picture/Integrating the parts/Creative, out-of-the-box	Focused/Differentiating the parts/Methodical, structured
5 Happiness	Inner-directed/Joy as a state of being	Outer-directed/The joy of achievement
6 Conflict resolution	Transforming the inner environment/Self-talk	Transforming the outer environment/Effective communication
7 People management	People-oriented/Coaching/Inspiring	Task-oriented/Mentoring/Delegating (in an empowering way)
8 Time management	Being in the now/Inner-directed/Long-term planning	Effective time management/Short term planning
9 Power	Power to attract desired outcomes from within	Power to take action toward desired outcomes/Inclusive power
10 Leadership	Transformational or Quiet leadership	Transactional leadership

I-F — — — — — — — — — — — — — — **I-M**

1 Oneself	Lack of self-awareness/Low self-esteem/Directionless	Self-defeating actions/Unable to bring things to fruition
2 Others	Relationships at all costs/Giving power away/Servile	Authoritarian/Sense of entitlement/Acts of conditional love
3 Knowing	Superstition/wishful thinking/High level, superficial view	Assuming logic to be the key to all knowing/Lost in the details
4 Thinking	All over the place/Broad, unintegrated thinking	Rigid, inflexible/Narrow reductionist "bottom-line" thinking
5 Happiness	Fun at all costs/Escapism/Addictions	Achievement at all costs/Workaholic
6 Conflict resolution	Mulling over/Self-doubt/Depression	Bulldozing over others/Bullying/Aggressive communication
7 People management	Needing to be liked/Subtly manipulative/Unassertive	Autocratic/Micromanaging/Do it my way
8 Time management	Unstructured/Procrastination/Lack of planning	Trying to fit too much in/Life dictated by the clock
9 Power	Disowns own power/Manipulative/Political maneuvering	Controlling/Overly competitive/"Power over" others
10 Leadership	Unassertive or Manipulative/Playing favorites	Autocratic/Command & control

Immature

- 159 -

Exploring the Model

The best way to get to know the model is to peruse it for a few minutes. Soon you will notice the interrelationships between each area within the four quadrants. You might even notice immediately where you tend to gravitate on the model.

In the next chapter you will have a chance to gauge where you tend to operate in the model by means of a questionnaire.

If you would like a more in-depth exploration of the model please refer to Appendix A, where the first two areas: *Relationship with Oneself* and *Relationship with Others* are discussed in detail. This will provide a deeper understanding of the model and how to interpret it, should you wish to have this.

Where Does Society Fit in the Model?

Currently most of the Western world arguably fits in the lower right quadrant although some of the more advanced cultures are already showing signs of operating in the mature half.

For more on this interesting topic and the evolution of society as shown on the model, please refer to Appendix B. There you will find a discussion on where Western society tends to fit on the model and how human cultures have evolved over time.

Five keys to working with the model

1. The goal is mature, balanced energy

The goal is to reach the upper half where we are embodying and expressing mature I-F and I-M. Once you have reached mature I-F, mature I-M is within easy reach.

2. Zig-zag tenet: the way up is across

We reach maturity in a specific area e.g. our capacity to nurture, by integrating some aspect of its complementary opposite energy.

When Henry Ford wanted to improve productivity from factory workers he didn't increase their working hours from 10 hours/day: he *decreased* them to eight hours/day. More downtime (I-F) improved productivity (I-M) by 10% across the board.

Here are some everyday examples:

- Brian is a manager who tends to be a little controlling and over-assertive in his management style (Immature I-M). To cultivate a more mature management style he needs to include more heart-based and intuitive capabilities. This could be achieved in different ways. One way is to allow others to participate in decisions and solutions and notice what happens. He could also practice listening to his intuition rather than forging ahead with logical next steps.
- Sue is a smart individual yet she often second-guesses herself and doubts her abilities (immature I-F). Sue could benefit by diving into her I-M: giving herself a project that she can handle, do some high level planning and then "just do it". She could continue giving herself stretch targets until she gets the gut knowing: "Hey, I can do things".
- Brittany tends to have a need to be liked and to be unassertive in her leadership style (Immature I-F). She could cultivate more "me-first" energy and learn to be more assertive with clearer boundaries in place (I-M). This would create an opportunity for her to become a transformational leader, one who can reach people on an emotional level and also remain focused on results.
- John has been working on starting a new business for the past few years but has not been able to bring it into fruition (immature I-M). Rather than just forging on he could benefit from a "return to self". He may have been backing the wrong horse – something he thought he "should" do rather than something he is truly

passionate about. He may have been trying too hard to forge ahead and not listening to the signals along the way. Outward successes that are joyful and sustainable (mature I-M) depend on taking action in alignment with your passion (I-F).

For more discussion on how an individual might navigate the way up using the zig-zag tenet, please refer to Appendix C, where four examples are described in greater detail.

3. *The gender binary keeps us in the immature half*

The more we conform to the gender binary and operate as halves, the more we operate in the immature zone.

It is impossible to operate in the mature zone and thrive with only half of your being. Whichever half is embodied – your masculine or I-F – you will necessarily operate from the immature half.

This is because you will automatically be operating from the "can only" space. A person *can only* think logically, but not intuitively or outside the box. They *can only* nurture, but not know when to stop and take care of their own needs. They *can only* work long, hard hours, but not know when to stop.

Yet, as we saw in chapter 8, we are still raising boys to be embody their masculine, macho energy and eschew their softer, feminine side.

We are still raising girls to serve and please others even if we also expect them to take on leadership roles and succeed in the world.

In many ways we are still raising children to be halves. This perpetuates a society in the immature half of the model. It is time for us to stop the misguided concept that the gender binary is something good, as though "nature intended it."

Nature intended us to evolve.

We need to see the gender binary for what it is: something that may have made sense sometime in the past but today, and for a while already, it has been a recipe for global imbalance and suffering.

4. In the immature half, life is a pendulum of extremes

One of the unavoidable consequences of operating as halves, and operating in the immature zone, is that life becomes a pendulum of extremes.

When we operate as halves, the suppressed parts of ourselves eventually find a way to come out, though usually not in a constructive way.

The workaholic might indulge in weekends of binge eating, drinking or doing drugs. During my workaholic phase my indulgence was chocolate. I still love chocolate and would never give it up but then I could eat a large slab in one night. It didn't affect my weight because I was running six days a week. Even then I knew with every fiber of my being that my busy lifestyle was simply masking an unhealthy habit – an addiction.

This was my feminine side crying out for attention. My unmet needs for comfort, nurturing and happiness was expressing itself and was "addressed" but only in an artificial way. Being unaddressed at its source, the need went unmet and this is what led to the binge eating.

When we're in the immature half of the model we are drawn to a relationship of two halves. This is also a recipe for extremes, where we might as well be from different planets! In this sense we experience extremes through our partner.

We project suppressed parts of ourselves onto our partner. Expectations are then created for *fulfilment by the other person*. In the course of doing this we give our power away. Resentments and fights ensue, constituting some version of "you owe me."

When we adhere to the gender binary we automatically operate in the immature half of the model. This necessitates that we fluctuate in extremes between our own I-M and I-F and we experience other extremes in our relationships.

5. In the mature half, life is a joyful creation

In the mature half we live from balanced energy.

Although the model depicts mature I-F and I-M as two distinct quadrants in the top half, these two areas interact in a harmonious and seamless way.

Hence the dotted line between the two upper quadrants in Figure 1.

Here, life is a joyful creation. The two energies are co-present and functional within us at all times.

Each is available to be drawn upon at will. As the ego is relaxed a higher spiritual intelligence (SQ) becomes enlivened, enabling the switching to happen automatically in response to situations requiring more I-F or I-M or a blend of both.

Each moment enables us to draw seamlessly from our mature I-F or I-M without having to consciously think about it. When this happens I-F and I-M operate synergistically, creating outcomes more beautiful and beneficial than the sum of the parts.

Delightfully, in the mature half, we are drawn to relationships of two whole persons. Here, the harmony and balance between I-F and I-M is naturally replicated on the outside as we relate to those aspects in our partner. For added discussion on relationships of two whole persons please see Appendix A.

CHAPTER 13

How Balanced Are You?

Knowing your state of inner balance is like having a roadmap that shows your next steps so that you can thrive in all areas of your life.

In this chapter you will be able to assess your own state of balance. There is no scoring here but rather questions that have been arranged according to 10 day-to-day areas of life such as *Relationship with Oneself, Relationship with Others*, etc. If there is an area that particularly draws your interest, you could start there.

The questionnaire is best done in a quiet, comfortable setting where you can connect with yourself as you allow the questions to settle into your awareness.

Simply go through the questions to get a sense of:

- Overall, do you tend to favor your I-M or I-F, or is it both?
- Among the 10 areas where do you feel good about yourself and where could you benefit from a tweak that will help you to thrive more?

As you go through the questions you can refer back to the model for reference if needed.

1. Relationship with Oneself

Relationship with Oneself: I-F Aspect

> *The overarching question is: "Do I relate to myself with awareness, sincerity, kindness, compassion, nurturing, love and trust?"*

1. Am I consciously aware of my feelings or needs in the moment and do I know what they pertain to?

    E.g. Knowing when I am feeling hungry, tired, sick, healthy, inspired, drained, rested, needing time alone, needing exercise, needing a break from working, needing to express myself or knowing when to do something to complete a project.

2. Do I accept myself as I am?
3. Do I feel love and compassion toward myself?
4. Am I able to forgive my past self?
5. Do I know when to nurture and take care of myself?
6. How well do I feel connected to my purpose/s?
7. Do I trust myself?
8. Do I take responsibility for how my life is turning out?

Relationship with Oneself: I-M Aspect

> *The overarching question is: "How well do I take care of my deepest needs through action?"*

1. Do I support myself in having what I need when I need it?

    E.g. Eating when hungry, eating healthily, resting when tired, doing the work I love, taking quiet time, getting regular exercise, giving myself time to play, taking time out, expressing myself when needed and taking timely action on the project.

2. Do my daily actions/habits support my health & wellbeing?
3. Am I self-motivated or do I need deadlines or other people to get me going?
4. Am I doing work that inspires and stretches me?
5. Am I taking steps to fulfill my purpose/s?
6. When necessary can I bring my projects to fruition through focus, will and action?
7. When I recognize that I need to improve my physical, emotional or mental health do I take the necessary steps to do so?
8. Do I feel competent and engaged in creating financial self-sufficiency?

2. Relationship with Others

Relationship with Others: I-F Aspect

> The overarching question is: "Can I connect with others from the heart, in a healthy way?"

1. Can I be in a relationship without giving away my power i.e. abandoning my own needs and making it all about the other person?
2. Can I be nurturing while still honoring my own needs and boundaries?
3. Do my own goals and dreams receive the attention they deserve or do I compromise on them based on the needs of others?
4. Do I maintain a healthy sense of self-esteem without needing my partner to instill it in me?
5. Am I comfortable that I (not others around me) am responsible for my own happiness?
6. Am I willing to leave an unhealthy relationship or is it "relationships at all costs"?
7. When I am with people do I manage my energy well or do I easily feel drained?
8. Do I nurture others when I am feeling rested and strong (as opposed to from a sense of duty regardless of how I am feeling)?

9. Can I be with powerful others without in some way giving my power away?

Relationship with Others: I-M Aspect

> The overarching question is: "Can I relate to others in a supportive and empowering way?"

1. Is my relationship behavior guided by having an empathic, caring attitude with a strong sense of self?
2. Do I relate to my partner as an equal rather than wanting to be dominant and "in charge"?
3. Do I support my partner in practical, tangible ways by doing whatever I can to help?
4. Am I empowering toward others?
5. Does my relationship support others to reach their own potential?
6. Do I willingly share household and other necessary chores?
7. Do I generously give my time and energy to help others with something they're working on – without necessarily expecting something in return?
8. Do I willingly impart knowledge and skills as opposed to hoarding it because "knowledge is power"?
9. Do I know when to let go of helping others to enable them to help and empower themselves?

3. Approach to Knowing

Approach to Knowing: I-F Aspect

> The overarching question is: "Can I rely on my inner guidance and receptivity to know what is true for me?"

1. Can I discern what my intuition is telling me even if it involves risk as opposed to just taking "the rational and sensible route"?

2. Does my own inner wisdom guide me more strongly than other people's views or social norms?
3. Do I gain insights and information based on what my body is telling me?
4. Do I pay attention to the synchronicities in my life and derive meaning and purpose from them?
5. In a meeting can I hear different inputs and take cognizance of the complexities, yet arrive at an overall, considered understanding of how best to move forward?

Approach to Knowing: I-M Aspect

> The overarching question is: "Can I use logic and reasoning as a discretionary tool to guide me toward positive and practical outcomes when needed?"

1. Can I effectively use logical reasoning to know what my next steps are?
2. Can I use logical reasoning in situations where it adds value as opposed to being over-reliant on it because of a belief that "logic is the key to all knowing"?
3. Do I have to think about how I'm feeling in order to know how I am feeling?
4. Can I analyze situations involving detail without getting lost in the detail? (e.g. would I make good decisions on the stock market after studying the detail?)
5. Can I break down a problem or situation into its constituent parts to help me know what to do next?

4. Approach to Thinking

Approach to Thinking: I-F Aspect

> The overarching question is: "Does my thinking enable me to gain a big picture view of a situation or to think creatively and out of the box when needed?"

1. Do I easily tune in to the broader implications of a decision e.g. how it might affect others?
2. As a consumer do I notice the potential impacts of a company or brand I purchase from on the environment or other stakeholders?
3. Do I tend to recognize patterns and trends?
4. During conversations am I able to integrate my own train of thoughts without getting lost and being "all over the place"?
5. Am I able to think out-of-the-box and provide creative solutions to problems?

Approach to Thinking: I-M Aspect

> *The overarching question is: "Can I utilize my thinking to gain a focused, detailed view of a situation or to think in a methodical and structured way when needed?"*

1. Can I focus on a project without getting lost in it e.g. skipping meals or appointments?
2. Can I develop expertise in my field without becoming narrow in my thinking? (e.g. a Western doctor being open alternative medicine?)
3. Can I think in methodical and structured ways when appropriate (e.g. on a project) but understand its limitations in other areas (e.g. in matters of the heart)?
4. Can I distinguish between "clear, logical thinking" e.g. to run a business efficiently, as opposed to "cold, bottom-line" thinking e.g. "profits at all costs"?
5. Can I value science without getting stuck in "nothing-is-real-unless-proven-scientifically" thinking?

5. Approach to Happiness

Approach to Happiness: I-F Aspect

> *The overarching question is: "Can I turn inward to find happiness without relying on the use of substances?"*

1. Do I experience joy as a state of being?
2. Am I able to cultivate joy within myself when I choose?
3. Do I find happiness from within as opposed to craving the fleeting happiness that comes from "getting stuff" - shopping, gambling, eating, drinking, smoking, drugs or TV?
4. Do I manage my stress in inner-directed ways such as meditation, breathing techniques or self-talk, rather than using forms of escapism like parties, drugs or comfort eating?

Approach to Happiness: I-M Aspect

> *The overarching question is: "Can I enjoy outer achievements and success without becoming dependent on those for my happiness?"*

1. Can I enjoy achievements at work without becoming a workaholic who is addicted to success?
2. Can I enjoy adventure or sport without becoming addicted to the "high" as an extreme sports fanatic or adrenaline junkie?
3. When I find myself in a phase of not achieving tangible or visible achievements I feel...

6. Approach to Conflict Resolution

Approach to Conflict Resolution: I-F Aspect

> *The overarching question is: "Can I turn inward to resolve conflict effectively?"*

1. After an argument can I reasonably move forward as opposed to mulling things over and over?
2. Can I restore my wellbeing by acknowledging my feelings "with no blame or shame" and working my way back to feeling good?
3. Am I able to experience and manage my inner environment – my thoughts and feelings?
4. Do I manage my anger constructively as opposed to turning it inwards (i.e. depression)?

5. Have I mastered the art of resolving a conflict with someone by first addressing it within myself rather than simply confronting them?

Approach to Conflict Resolution: I-M Aspect

> The overarching question is: "Can I turn outward and resolve conflict effectively?"

1. Do I communicate calmly in a conflicted situation, as opposed to being aggressive?
2. Do I communicate assertively without bulldozing over, or interrupting others?
3. Do I communicate in such a way as to give both parties the benefit of the doubt, and leave the integrity of each party intact?
4. Do I manage my anger constructively as opposed to turning my anger outwards (i.e. aggression)?
5. Can I influence others to calm down?

7. Approach to People Management

Approach to People Management: I-F Aspect

> The overarching question is: "Can I manage people toward business outcomes by awakening their own inherent motivation, confidence and potential?"

1. Can I coach and inspire my employees to grow in their role?
2. Can I have friendly relationships at work and maintain healthy boundaries?
3. Can I foster good relationships with my employees without becoming unassertive and people-pleasing?
4. Can I be inspiring and approachable without allowing others to take advantage of me?
5. Can I assess each employee fairly (based on merit, for example) or do I play favorites?

Approach to People Management: I-M Aspect

> *The overarching question is: "Can I manage people toward business outcomes by channeling and growing their skillset via tasks and actions?"*

1. Do I share knowledge and skills with my employees in order to empower them toward their potential or do I hoard knowledge?
2. Am I an effective mentor as opposed to merely being autocratic?
3. Would I mentor an employee even if they could potentially grow into my job role?
4. Can I delegate in a way that is empowering to others, not just giving orders?
5. Can I manage people without micromanaging them?

8. Approach to Time Management

Approach to Time Management: I-F Aspect

> *The overarching question is: "Can I manage my time optimally by being self-referring?"*

1. Am I able to be present in the moment?
2. Do I get a clear inner sense of when the time is right for a particular action (e.g. calling someone on the phone) thus helping me be in the flow of my life?
3. Do I have a sense of timing as opposed to being unstructured and random with my use of time?
4. When I have a lot on my "to-do list" can I tune in to get a sense of what feels like the best "next step"?

Approach to Time Management: I-M Aspect

> *The overarching question is: "Can I manage my time optimally by working effectively with clock time?"*

1. Do I arrive on time for meetings and appointments?
2. Do I use a clock for time management without my life being dictated by the clock?
3. Do I calmly and purposefully attend to my day's activities without being in a perpetual rush?
4. Do I accept what can reasonably be done in a day without "pushing the envelope" and trying to fit in more?

9. Approach to Power

Approach to Power: I-F Aspect

> The overarching question is: "Can I attain desired outcomes from within by mastering the Law of Attraction?"

1. Do I "own" my personal power (i.e. being self-possessed) or do I give my power away in order to be liked by others?
2. Do I consciously create the conditions within myself (e.g. clear intentions, heart-centered powerful vision, etc.) to attract positive outcomes?
3. Do I know how to manage my thoughts and feelings positively so that I can be in the right space to receive what I have requested?
4. Can I attract what I want without emotionally manipulating others to get it?

Approach to Power: I-M Aspect

> The overarching question is: "Can I attain desired, beneficent outcomes by taking effective, empowering action myself or through others?"

1. Can I get things done through my own determination and action?
2. Do I use my power to contribute toward a better world rather than just to appease the ego?

3. Do I know how to get things done through action when needed as opposed to struggle and hard work as a way of life?
4. Do I use my status and position to empower others?

   When involving others, do I use my formal power inclusively and to seek win-win outcomes or do I use it autocratically as "power over" others?

10. Approach to Leadership

Approach to Leadership: I-F Aspect

> The overarching question is: "Can I lead myself and others through emotional intelligence and heartfelt connections?"

1. Am I comfortable using an emotionally intelligent leadership style (such as Transformational Leadership) as opposed to merely a people-pleasing style?
2. Do I know how to inspire and connect with others without losing sight of the desired outcomes?
3. Am I comfortable in my leadership role as opposed to being bashful and unassertive?
4. Do I know how to engage in a people-oriented style of leadership without resorting to manipulation or favoritism?

Approach to Leadership: I-M Aspect

> The overarching question is: "Can I lead myself and others by focusing effectively on tasks and strategic thinking?"

1. Am I comfortable using a task-focused leadership style (such as Transactional Leadership) when needed as opposed to being excessively results-driven?
2. Do I empower others as opposed to laying down the law of how things should be done?

3. Is my leadership aimed at win-win situations or is it about improving the quality of my life or my business even if it comes at the expense of others?
4. Do I consciously use my leadership position for good or do I crave the security of feeling in charge?

Congratulations on completing the questionnaire. This should give you an idea of your overall state of balance.

It should also give you an idea of a specific area or two where you might wish to cultivate greater balance and thus pave the way for more thriving in this area.

Making the shift will not only help you to thrive in that particular area but in others too. A benefit in one area tends to spill over into other parts of your life. It is all connected.

CHAPTER 14

Seven Steps to Balance

Now that you know how balanced you are, it is time for action. Here is a seven-step process that will help you to become more balanced and whole.

By doing so you will naturally attract and create more success in your personal life, your relationships and your career. As mentioned in the beginning of this book, this is what I call the *Law of Balance*.

These are easy steps to follow and you should soon see tangible results. For best results, give yourself time to carry out each step thoroughly before moving on.

Step 1: Awareness

Acknowledge to yourself that you have both I-M and I-F. Make peace with this idea. This seemingly small step is the crucial foundation for the rest of the process.

For many this involves rethinking limiting beliefs about who we are and being willing to move past conditioning. For some this may be a relatively easy step. It may be an idea you are already comfortable with.

Either way, allow yourself to be present with the idea that you have I-M and I-F. Let it settle into your awareness. Affirm that it is safe to acknowledge both sides of yourself.

Tune into the "signature feeling" of each side. This helps you to recognize your I-F and I-M. To assist with this, you might reflect back on your day or week. Notice where you were in your I-F and where you were in your I-M.

You might also go back to the guided meditation at the end of chapter 2 and use that to tune into your I-F and I-M.

This first step – acknowledging and connecting with sides of yourself – is like turning the key in the ignition. It is the start of a new journey. It unleashes energy that was previously kept at bay.

Pay attention to your dreams. You may receive interesting insights.

It is time to open up to who you really are. Make the decision to step forward and honor the beauty and fullness of who you are.

Step 2: Audit

Identify your current state of balance. The Journey-to-Balance Model helps to achieve this outcome.

Identify:

- Whether you operate from your I-M or your I-F, or both
- Where your "center of gravity" lies – in which quadrant or half
- Specific areas you may wish to balance or mature

If you feel you may be biased in your self-assessment, ask one or more friends for their input. You may get consistent feedback in certain areas, which can be helpful for creating a more accurate "audit."

Step 3: Identify

Identify an area you would like to enhance.

Consider what the model revealed. To arrive at one or two areas confirm the best choice by asking yourself: "Where do I tend to struggle repeatedly?" or "What do I most want to shift within myself?"

For example, if this were me ten years ago when I worked in a corporate environment I would want to enhance my management style. I wanted to be a really good manager. However, I found myself inadvertently taking the reins too much at times, particularly when I felt the need to protect my own team from untimely demands from other departments. This meant that I resorted to the lower right quadrant when stressed. If I had seen this model then, I would have known instantly where to focus my energies: developing a more heart-spaced, inclusive and cooperative management style.

I would also have wanted to work on identifying a deeper purpose and take steps toward it, something I felt I lacked at that time.

Step 4: Visualize

Visualize the very thing you want to achieve within yourself. In my previous example it would be seeing myself as a balanced and effective manager who can maintain the relationships yet still honor certain boundaries. It would also be imagining what it would feel like to live my life on purpose, doing the work I love and contributing my gifts to the world (that would have taken a career change, as it turns out).

Here are questions to consider:

- How would I feel if this area was no longer a struggle?
- What would life be like once I bring this area into maturity?
- How would achievement in this area impact other parts of my life?

If I had managed to bring my management style to the next level by cultivating a balance of mature I-M and I-F in that specific area, I would have felt a quiet confidence in myself and derived more pleasure from the job. That could have spilled over into other areas, such as my relationship with myself and with others outside of work. Identify these potential spin-off benefits.

Step 5: Choose

Choose some possible avenues for achieving a particular desired outcome.

What does your gut tell you?

The first step is asking: what is the most effective way forward? Refer first to your gut feeling about this. It can also help to consider these guidelines:

Be guided by the zig-zag tenet of the Model

We covered the zig-zag tenet in chapter 12: If you find yourself operating from an immature I-M or I-F quality and you want to shift into the mature version, focus on the complementary opposite area for your solution.

In the example of my management style I would immediately know that I needed to bring in more I-F so that I could bring my tendency to be controlling and overprotective – both immature I-M qualities – up into the mature half. That is the general strategy based on the zig-zag tenet.

The next question is: specifically, what would I be, or do, to bring in more I-F? In the context of my situation I would have focused on bringing more heart into my relationships at work.

I could begin by asking my team how I could support them rather than stepping in to protect them when tough demands were made on their time by others. Another would have been to go back to basics within myself – to touch base with what I most wanted to achieve in my role as manager and practice using intentionality, visualization and the energy of love (the Law of Attraction) to manifest it. You might have your own ideas about how to attain this.

A third element would have been to trust the process more, to "let go" more and let things play out, while being more collaborative with the other department managers who needed support from my team. Had I tried this option, I feel I would have had a positive response from everyone involved.

Create a specific intervention

Using the zig-zag tenet, what is something you can do to cultivate more of the opposite pole energy in yourself?

Examples

- If you tend to be nurturing at your own expense practice applying your boundaries more firmly by saying "no" when you observe yourself giving too much.
- If you tend to be a micromanager with your employees at work practice focusing on relationship-building with them by learning to listen more and practice empathy with them.
- If you tend to rely too much on outer achievements in order to feel happy, try cultivating happiness as a state of being perhaps by taking a course in mindfulness meditation.

These are examples of specific interventions but there is no "one right way" of doing it.

Create a non-specific intervention

With reference to the zig-zag tenet, a non-specific intervention means cultivating any aspect of the opposite pole energy to enliven that side of yourself.

Just by cultivating the complementary opposite pole – even in a non-specific way – you are automatically contributing toward your solution.

- *If you need to cultivate more I-F* find any way to cultivate it e.g. if you tend to work relentlessly you might join a meditation class, get a cat, go for a massage, spend time in the garden or practice listening without giving solutions.
- *If you need to cultivate more I-M* find any way to do this e.g. if you find it hard to say "no", do anything that cultivates I-M such as giving yourself an achievable DIY project and enjoying the completion of it, challenging yourself to say "yes" to an opportunity to speak publicly, doing something just for yourself (i.e. put yourself first) or standing up to a person who you feel is undermining you in some way.

Relax gender roles

Participate in a role that was previously thought to be "not yours" – such as for cooking, cleaning, taking out the garbage, driving the car, doing the finances, paying for meals, gardening, doing DIY projects, fetching the kids from school or shopping.

Do more of whatever you thought was for the opposite sex. Do it with the support of your partner by explaining to him/her what this means to you and why this would be healthy for you as well as your relationship. The reason this step is important is it gives you daily opportunities to experience your "opposite sex" energy. Becoming balanced is after all, not just a new mindset. It is about practicing and experiencing.

Step 6: Action

By now you have a desired outcome and you have identified various ways in which to achieve it. Ensure you have given thought to where and when you plan to carry out these interventions e.g. "during weekly staff meetings" or "every morning" or "when I get home from work."

Now it's time to take action. Give yourself time to experience your various interventions. As you go along, monitor the results and adjust your strategy if necessary.

Example

- Keep a journal of the mature quality you intend to cultivate
- Write down your strategy for attaining this
- Build this into your daily and weekly routine
- Take action
- Monitor how it goes and adjust the strategy if necessary
- If something is not working, try an alternative route

Step 7: Live!

Finally, it is time to recognize your newfound capabilities as you grow, and celebrate the new, more effective you!

Watch as you become effective in areas of previous limitation.

There is little quite as rewarding as growing in self-mastery and gradually becoming more fully who you are.

CHAPTER 15

A New Paradigm

By getting to know and experience yourself as a whole being with a healthy, enlivened I-M and I-F, you have created the conditions for you to thrive. You now have the key to happiness and abundance in all the major areas of your life – wherever you choose it to be.

Stepping into your own fullness is also an enormous contribution to the world. It is doing your part in co-creating a new era of balance and harmony, what the world is yearning for. You are contributing positively to this simply by being who you are.

We have already begun to enter the new era even if collectively we are still grappling with – and in the process of letting go of – the old paradigm. The polarization we see in the world today is part of the journey. Like moments prior to the sudden shift of the earth's crust in an earthquake, resistance is at its highest. This is to be expected.

Resistance is there because "the rules of the game" are changing – and fast. Consider how our understanding of good leadership has changed in the past two decades. The old command-and-control style may have its uses during dire circumstances but as a general way of leading it is a dinosaur. Relationship-building and emotional intelligence are now recognized as crucial skills for today's leaders.

This is part of the feminine being restored into the mainstream of life, an example of what characterizes the new era.

The next step: effortless being

This book has shown that it is possible to be balanced while in a physical body. Not only is it possible, it is what we are meant to be. It is in *this* state that we can become channels for Source to express divine potential through us. This is how we bring "heaven on earth."

It is what all religions and spiritual paths have ushered us toward by encouraging us to be good. This book brings us to the same desired outcome – not by being good – but by being balanced.

When balanced, our inner compass cannot help but guide us in directions and endeavors that are for the highest good of all. When we are balanced our masculine side cannot help but work in alignment with the wisdom of the inner compass.

This is where effortless being also comes into play. Having what you want is less about struggle and the effort of having to do it all yourself. It is more about attending to and nurturing that beautiful inner state of balance and utilizing it. This is your center, your core. It is also your point of attraction for everything that comes into your life.

We no longer need to spend enormous amounts of time and energy in the process of learning who we are *by learning who we are not*. That way of learning, which involved suffering, belonged to the preceding polarized eras.

What it looks like

When inner balance is there necessary actions emerge spontaneously.

This is what Taoists refer to as *Wu Wei* or "non-action." It's not passivity. It is action that flows as a natural extension of your being – not through effort or struggle. Your actions are effortlessly in alignment with the flow of life just as the planets revolve around the sun without effort and struggle.

To this end, Lao Tzu wrote:

> *Less and less do you need to force things,*
> *Until finally you arrive at non-action.*

> *When nothing is done,*
> *Nothing is left undone.*

For minds stuck in logical thinking, this is a complete riddle. For those open to intuitive thinking it is clear.

It is what Jeshua alluded to: *"Consider the lilies, how they grow: they neither toil nor spin."* The lilies do not revert to the use of the egoic will and effort to have their needs met. Their doing comes from the effortlessness of being in the flow.

The same is available to us. I believe this is what life is meant to be.

Balancing every day

Until inner balance is a habitual way of being you will need to reinforce and support it. It takes time to unlearn our conditioning and it takes continued focus to become balanced amid a society that does not yet understand or champion it.

To support yourself reinforce your balance every day. Metaphysics states that "where attention goes, energy flows." This keeps the state of balance enlivened until it becomes a natural state of being.

When you wake up, take a little time to acknowledge and celebrate your I-M and I-F energies. You could do this at other times in the day too such as when standing in a queue or waiting for an appointment. If you prefer, you could communicate and develop a more intimate relationship with your I-M and I-F as per the guided meditation at the end of chapter two.

Heal the problem through balance

Remember the phrase: "Show me a problem and I'll show you a masculine-feminine imbalance"?

Doing "the balance test" is a useful yardstick in any situation that is not going well. It can be used in every aspect of your life including your relationship with yourself, relationships with others and work. Simply ask yourself: does this situation represent too much masculine energy or too much feminine energy? What does it need now?

Here is a simple example. When I was nearly finished writing this book I discovered that my eyes had taken strain due to the amount of computer time involved. By not taking enough breaks during the writing process I had strained my eyes. This is too much I-M – working relentlessly until the job is done. Now I realize I need to pay attention to my body and give it the necessary breaks it needs (I-F).

Recognizing personal, interpersonal and global problems as manifestations of imbalance is truly empowering. It takes the guesswork away and provides a useful indication of what is needed. It gets straight to the heart of the problem and enables a solution to be created at the source rather than wasting time and money trying to control the symptoms.

For example, the global drug problem is an attempted short cut to happiness. What if children and teens were taught how to deal with their emotions and create happiness from within? This would give many a way out before it gets to the point that drugs seem the only viable way to feel good and deal with the emptiness within.

A shift in consciousness (awareness of how to deal with the problem) can mean a large shift in outer circumstances.

This is how we can heal a problem using "the balance test" rather than fighting it at the level of outward appearances or symptoms, which just fosters its persistence.

Living the new value

One of the ways to usher in the new era of balance and harmony is to integrate its values. At its most basic level it means avoiding the perpetuation of stereotypes.

Being a role model

Ralph Waldo Emerson said "What you do speaks so loud that I cannot hear what you say."

One of the greatest contributions you can make to this planet at this time is being a role model for inner balance.

This will not only assist children but people of all ages. By giving yourself permission to be who you are beyond a gender stereotype, you are unconsciously giving permission to others to be who they are. They then have the "luxury" of relaxing, letting go of their masks, and being true to the deeper side of their nature.

Raising children to be balanced

The new paradigm requires a rethinking of the way we raise children or influence other people's children through our interactions with them.

Children learn by observation so the first task in creating balanced children is that we ourselves must become balanced.

As a parent who adheres to the gender binary it is of little use to tell boys that it's OK to be nurturing and have feelings, and tell girls that it's OK to cultivate ambition and play with action men. It has to be backed up through our own behavior. Boys need to see men taking responsibility for domestic chores and child raising in order to see that it is OK to do the same.

Being a good role model also entails awareness of what we say. Initially as we are unlearning our own conditioning we may catch ourselves saying something like: "Since you're a girl you might want the princess outfit" or "Stop crying Johnny. Be a man."

We need to be conscious role models because conditioning creeps in at an early age. I have heard that babies as young as one year of age can already recognize gendered behavior.

Paulo, the entrepreneur who underwent his own journey to balance, urged:

> *We've got to encourage that opening up to inner balance earlier. If you leave it too late it's more difficult. When you're younger you take more risks. If this comes into your life earlier you have more time to explore it and play with it and find your truth. If you leave it for later, you will find it more difficult because you have the pressure*

> *of time and other pressures against you. You're more set in your ways.*

While it's good to ask a child what toy they want to play with, remember that programming starts at a very young age and it comes from other influences too – school, religion, games and the media. Children as young as one or two could already be conditioned and not even know it.

Go further by making it fun and impressive to explore both sides of themselves.

Actively encourage balance. As Paulo says, "Tell boys it is OK to play rugby but it's just as OK to paint a picture." The same applies to girls: "It's OK to be nurturing and kind, but it's just as OK to be president – and to speak assertively during your campaign."

Using inclusive language

Referring to Source

The new era requires that every human being, regardless of gender or sexual orientation, is afforded the dignity, comfort and self-esteem that come with the acknowledgement that Source is both masculine and feminine.

God's masculine image is a projection of patriarchal thinking. We owe it to ourselves and the generations to come to move past this harmful notion by referring to God with gender neutral pronouns.

Reverend Michael Bernard Beckwith of the Agape Church in Los Angeles uses the pronouns "it" or "God's" such as "we are God's children" and "God showed its love to the world." I discovered that hearing it this way is absolutely fine. It may be something to get used to at first but it becomes utterly natural. It is inclusive. Everybody is acknowledged, nobody is excluded because of a one-sided view of life.

Referring to Animals

The new era calls upon us to refrain from using default masculine pronouns for animals. We can no longer with a clear conscience display such biased attention and acknowledgement of one gender as though it were "the default."

A bird, squirrel, sea creature or any other animal should be referred to in gender neutral terms unless it is specifically known to be male or female. Rather than saying: "Oh look, isn't he magnificent?" simply say "Oh look, isn't it a magnificent bird?" We need to realize that creating separation and division lead to bias and suffering. This approach has no place in the new era which is about equality, inclusivity and genuine progress.

A call to action!

Discussion groups

A great way to grow toward balance is by creating or participating in a discussion group that focuses on the desired transformation and acts as a means to "unpack" it into bite-sized chunks.

One of the most powerful experiences I've ever had was participating in a dream studies group: we met every two weeks. Each member would take a turn to share a dream and then invite questions and discussion about that dream. Those sharing their interpretations would honor the one sharing his or her dream by saying "if it were my dream, I would… ("see the dove as a symbol for peace," to give an example). This was very powerful. A similar approach could be applied here.

No individual was an expert but everyone had taken the same basic course and had a common language and understanding. It was then up to each individual to share their wisdom and insights in the group.

The same concept can be applied to discussion groups focused on cultivating inner balance. Each session could address a particular theme or an area of challenge by having one or two people share personal stories. It could then be opened up for similarly respectful discussion and insights.

Blogs and chat rooms

Another way to stimulate discussion and share ideas is via a blog or chat room. This is a great way to get your ideas shared with people from all over the world. Pose a question, combined with a real life story to your blog and ask for inputs.

Making this a regular feature helps to create momentum and interest. Since the idea of gender fluidity is new to many people, you may find that it stirs controversy.

Using this book as a guide

Use this book as a guide for yourself or in a discussion group. Once you have read the book, you can return to certain chapters to focus on refining your understanding.

Allow yourself to do the questionnaire at least twice a year. This serves as a yardstick to gauge your progress.

Writing articles

If you are a writer or an aspiring writer, why not bring your talents forth to help usher in the new era of balance and harmony? You could potentially reach hundreds or even thousands of people. By expressing the ideas in this book as well as your own ideas, you are helping to spread joy around the planet.

Be yourself and thrive

Congratulations for coming to this new appreciation of yourself.

The awareness you have gained places you in a unique position to create success on many levels in your life. This is not only about the outer achievements but equally about the inner achievements – the shifts in mindset, the overcoming of obstacles and the healing (making whole) along the way.

This is true success. This is why we incarnate into physical reality – to experience, grow and create anew.

Enjoy the journey! May you be blessed with the fullness of who you are so that you can thrive now and in the new era.

APPENDIX A

Discussing the First Two Areas of the Model

This discussion provides additional information that might be helpful for understanding the model in greater depth. It covers *Relationship with Oneself* and *Relationships with Others*. It does not cover the other eight areas due to space limitations.

1. Relationship with Oneself

Relationship with Oneself: I-F Aspect

When it comes to your relationship with yourself the I-F has four main elements: self-awareness, self-esteem, self-love and being in touch with your sense of purpose.

All four elements need to be developed to a mature level to have mastered I-F in this area.

It is a real challenge to develop maturity in these areas given the pressures of living in a fast-paced, outward-oriented society.

Moreover, it is often said: "we are hardest on ourselves." That is why *this* particular relationship is not easy to master.

Yet our relationship with ourselves is the most important one we can have. Everything else is affected by this starting point, including our relationships with others.

> *In fact, your I-F component of your relationship with yourself is the single most important element in this entire model.*

This is the original domino that plays out and affects every other area in the model.

It affects the way you express ourselves in the world (the I-M aspect of your relationship with self). It is also the basis for how you relate to others, your happiness and success. It affects everything including your home and family life, your career, your ability to work with people and your ability to create positive outcomes.

All of this starts with your relationship with yourself.

Relationship with Oneself: I-M Aspect

This is the expressed part of your relationship with yourself.

This is the part that is visible to the world. It is about how much you actively support and express yourself in ways that are positive and constructive. When this part is mature, it is working in alignment with mature I-F.

For example, when you feel hungry, do you eat? When you feel tired, do you get rest? If you have a project to complete, do you get into action and complete it (or do you procrastinate)? If you feel the need to be heard, do you speak up?

Your needs represent your I-F. The degree to which you take action to satisfy them is your I-M.

The best way to operate from mature I-M is to ensure that your actions are in alignment with your needs and desires as identified by your mature I-F.

Taking little to no action to support your needs, taking actions that thwart your chances of success or taking actions that are purely ego-driven are immature I-M actions.

Relationship with Oneself: What Balance Is Like

Balance is taking action in alignment with your deepest desires, one of the best ways to experience heaven on earth.

Your I-F provides the compass, inputs, understanding, knowing or the feeling of what is needed now. Your I-M provides a physical, tangible means of satisfying your needs through aligned effort and action.

> *I once heard the story of a busy professional woman whom I will call Sam, who began to have chronic low energy and poor digestion. With no idea what the problem was she was concerned that it may be something quite serious. She went to see a Chinese doctor hoping to find answers. After giving her a check-up he turned to her and said: "Your body is tired. You need to sleep."*

It is as simple as that. Tune in. Listen to your body and what it is telling you about your emotional, physical and spiritual needs. Then take the necessary action to give yourself what you need and bring these into fruition.

Sam was all about work and action (I-M), but had neglected her own needs (I-F). This behavior falls into the immature half.

When Sam saw how simple the solution was it gave her an opening to reconnect to herself and give herself what she needs. It may not always be easy but this is the challenge.

Relationship with Oneself: What Imbalance Is Like

What is this like? It is living with unfulfilled needs.

If I-F is not yet enlivened within us, we don't really know who we are or what we want. We can take action and be busy but it lacks meaning and fulfilment. We may then find ourselves searching for yet another exciting experience or distraction. This is because of lacking the inner guidance and peace that comes through I-F.

Being overly-identified with one's masculine side sets up the conditions for: "all action, no real direction." We then get into action for its own sake – anything to keep moving.

We might eat on the run or skip meals because we are out of touch with our inner promptings. We might get caught up in working long hours, habitually overriding the body's needs for food and rest.

When we finally take a vacation we don't quite know what to do with ourselves because we don't know how to "just be." With all the activity there may be some hit and miss moments of excitement and satisfaction but they are not lasting. Our need to stay busy is fueled by a habitual preference for action and a need for entertainment or achievement to avoid feeling empty inside.

Without a healthy self-regard (which we gain through the I-F aspect of relating to ourselves) we may end up unconsciously sabotaging ourselves and thwarting our chances of success. This is where we can become our own worst enemy, inadvertently tripping ourselves up.

> *Once I agreed to provide pro-bono coaching to a young woman who was eager to graduate from high school and go on to further studies so that she could lift herself out of poverty and create a better life than her parents were able to.*
>
> *We made excellent strides in the first two sessions. On the third session she didn't show up.*
>
> *My schedule was tight so I was a little annoyed. I called her to find out what had happened. She had decided the night before that she would honor another appointment that had suddenly came up that day, instead of our coaching session. She had not telephoned or texted me. This is sabotaging oneself.*

On a day-to-day level we might trip ourselves up simply by eating junk food or otherwise engaging in unhealthy habits. This is because we are not receiving the inner guidance from the I-F and that is because we have either suppressed it or have not yet opened up to it. When this happens we typically have a lot of unresolved feelings that need to be addressed before we can truly "hear" the subtle promptings of the mature I-F, the inspired inner guidance system. This entails accepting that we have feelings and learning healthy ways of releasing them.

Similarly, if we are over-identified with our I-F (and I-M is not functional) we might very well *know* what we wish for but it remains just that: wishful thinking. We do not follow through with action. We lack the courage to make our own needs *that* important. This is a frustrating place to be because we all yearn for self-expression in the world, for a sense of fulfilment, yet in this scenario we can't seem to get ourselves going.

Operating from the immature half also means we tend to swing from one extreme to the other. We might try to "balance" our work fatigue by drinking too much coffee or through letting off steam through excessive partying. While this might seem to address the problem in the short term, it turns out not to bring lasting satisfaction.

The key to a happy and successful life is to establish a healthy relationship with yourself by acknowledging and enlivening your I-F and I-M and allowing them to work in alignment.

After all, this is an area of life we can all do something about. We cannot change other people or the weather or the financial climate but we can change ourselves and the way we operate.

2. Relationship with Others

Relationship with Others: I-F Aspect

On a day-to-day level the I-F approach to relationships with others is about emotionally connecting with them, being able to empathize with their needs and feeling love for them.

This love often expresses itself through a deep sense of connection, a desire to nurture, to have patience, acceptance and enjoyment, a desire to be of service and to make others comfortable and happy.

"Relationship with others" applies to romantic relationships and those with family, children, friends and colleagues. The questionnaire and discussion focus on intimate relationships.

These are really two questions: the first is "Am I able and comfortable to connect with others from the heart?"

The second is "Can I connect with others in a healthy way so as not to over-give and deplete myself in the process?" The mature I-F way of relating to others is about connecting from the heart without being a doormat.

Relationship with Others: I-M Aspect

The mature masculine aspect of your relationship with others is the part that is enacted and expressed in visible ways often through acts of kindness and service. This is about translating your feelings into tangibles: action and results.

"Empowering others" as a way of relating is key. Empowering others is an act of love as opposed to controlling others, diminishing them or using them for selfish gain. In a work situation this could be empowering others with knowledge. In an intimate relationship it is about relating as equals despite possible differences between the two individuals.

It is also about sharing the weight of all responsibilities. Not sharing household chores, for example, is a clear instance of immature I-M playing out in a relationship.

The distinction between doing acts of service for others from a mature I-M vs. from an immature I-M is that the former is done willingly and selflessly whereas the latter is done as a bargaining chip (you do this for me, I do that for you).

The key to graduating into the mature half is transcending the need to put ego first.

This is also really two questions: "Can I benefit the other person at all, as opposed to sitting back and looking out for "number one"?" Secondly, "Can I relate in a way that supports and empowers the other and does not resort to a coercive or "power over" relationship?"

Relationship with Others: What Balance Is Like

When I-F and I-M are internally balanced we are able to have a loving and mutually empowering relationship with another person. Our partner is our equal even if there are differences between us.

The I-F provides the empathy, the caring – the heart connection. This part is openly shared. The I-M provides tangible aspects in the form of doing things. This could include providing financial support, doing domestic chores, running errands or doing projects at home. It also covers the structure of the relationship and contractual aspects.

When both aspects are embodied each partner is whole and complete. There is no "leader" or "follower" in such relationships yet each person may at times take the lead because of being more experienced in a certain area. Yet, even so, there is no "ownership" of certain areas or roles. There is a fluidity. There are no strict gender roles and each person adopts aspects of both roles.

There may be occasions when the partners mutually agree to go into different roles for a period, for example, when children are young or one spouse takes time off to pursue higher education or start a business while the other supports him or her. That is quite OK because it is a desired project rather than a fixed role that becomes confused with one's very identity.

To operate from a place of balance it is necessary to have reached maturity in both I-F and I-M aspects of relationships. However, to cultivate the mature I-M it is necessary to have the mature I-F aspect first. This is the next step for millions of people on the planet.

How can we be supportive and generously empowering of others (mature I-M) without the heart-space enlivened? A person who has not enlivened their mature I-F can only relate in ways that are about doing and finding a sense of security through structure and hierarchy (wanting to be the "alpha" person in the household). Such an individual will not feel comfortable with vulnerability (commonly mistaken for weakness) and will therefore not be comfortable showing feelings or allowing true intimacy.

In romantic relationships, when we balance our I-M and I-F we are able to relate to others empathically, yet from a strong sense of self with healthy boundaries intact. We're able to carry forth this mature heart-space into our actions and into the way we relate to one another as equals. We no longer need the other person to "complete us." We are already complete by ourselves.

Relationship with Others: What Imbalance Is Like

This represents the classical "relationships of two halves."

If the immature I-M aspect of relationships is dominant, we would not be able to do things for others from an open heart. That automatically relegates us into immature territory.

We would tend to relate to others from a competitive place and habitually resort to "power over" dynamics. Feelings and gentleness would be confused with weakness.

There would be a habitual need to control people and situations and to serve one's own needs – for example helping others but really doing it just to look good.

If the immature I-F aspect is dominant it means that we tend to be in "relationships at all costs." We tend to give our power to others just for the sake of being in a relationship.

This dynamic is easy to see in personal relationships where one person gives their power away and in extreme situations might stay in an abusive relationship just for the sake of being in a relationship, with all the imagined, yet illusionary security that comes with this.

In order to master our relationships with others we need to master our relationship with ourselves. Remember the domino effect?

The truth is it is impossible to be loving and open and have healthy boundaries if we are coming from a place of chronic low self-esteem. As soon as low self-esteem or insecurity kicks in the ego kicks in. When that happens we cannot love unconditionally or relate to others without attempting to gratify our ego-based sense of deficiency in some way.

Attempts to dominate and control are misguided I-M attempts to relieve the pain of insecurity. Attempts to be in relationship no matter what the cost are misguided I-F attempts to relieve the pain of insecurity. So once again it all begins with your relationship with yourself.

APPENDIX B

Society's Journey to Balance

While it is possible for societies to operate all over the model, the focus has been on the bottom right quadrant for the past few thousand years, particularly in the West.

Progressive societies such as the Scandinavian countries, Germany, Canada and New Zealand have arguably made strides toward the mature half of the model. The easiest way to gauge where a society operates is to look at its economic health and technological advancement in combination with its humanitarian and environmental practices.

Developing countries with an emphasis on tribal culture and a communal sense of identity, including many historical cultures, tend to operate in the bottom left.

This is where relationships, collectivism, "being raised by a village," tribal lore, a sense of connectedness to everything, superstition, rites and rituals play out. Life can be relatively peaceful within a tribe, however, not a lot of individual choices are available. As a result of the strong collectivistic identification with "my tribe", tribal skirmishes are nevertheless commonplace. Little technology is present in this quadrant.

Nevertheless, the bottom right is arguably where many countries in the world now find themselves, and from which we are now emerging. We are evolving from this but as the daily news shows, we have not left it.

The bottom right depicts unbalanced I-M where individuality, hierarchy, action, power, analytical reasoning and outer achievement are revered so highly that they are regarded as the "default way to be."

In this quadrant the tendency is to be oriented toward the outer world, to that which we can "see, touch and feel."

This is the quadrant where science and technology were introduced to the world, something that greatly benefits our everyday lives. However, it is also the realm where technology is still focused on functionality and the bottom line rather than also on the health and wellbeing of humans and the environment. This most desirable combination is only possible in the mature half of the model.

We previously explored how cell phone companies produce excellent technology, but much like the cigarette companies of old, they are ignoring the evidence of health hazards due to electromagnetic radiation. Frank Clegg, former president of Microsoft Canada and founder of *Canadians 4 Safe Technology*, indicates that overexposure to cell phones and wireless technology can damage our health (89). Research has shown that radiation from cell phones and Wi-Fi causes diminished reaction time in children, decreased motor function, increased distraction, hyperactivity and inability to focus on complex and long-term tasks (89).

The evidence of health-related risks to overexposure is inconvenient to the bottom line profitability of these companies and yet there are relatively inexpensive solutions available. This one-sided focus on functionality and the bottom-line is bottom-right thinking.

Not surprisingly the bottom right quadrant is where we would also expect to find patriarchy, colonialism, war, violence, slavery, autocratic leadership, corporate greed, factory farming and animal testing. Each of these has a utilitarian goal in mind and the ends justifies the means.

As mentioned before, this is not due to "evil" but is a predictable outcome of rampant and unbalanced I-M.

Society's journey to balance

The journey to balance and wholeness happens in three stages. Societies begin in the lower left (A), in what Ken Wilber (90) calls the *Pre-Personal Era*.

Figure 2: Collective journey to maturity and balance

Mature

C2:
Healthy, self-supporting actions/Able to bring things to fruition
Partner as equal/Supportive, empowering, loving behavior
Logic/Detailed knowledge of the parts
Focused/Differenti...
Outer-directed/The...
Transforming the o... ctive communication
Task-oriented/Ment... an empowering way)
Effective time management... term planning
Power to take action toward desired outcomes/Inclusive power
Transactional leadership

C1:
Self-awareness/Self-esteem/Self-love/Sense of purpose
Empathic, caring relationships from a strong sense of self
Intuition/Body/Holistic, integrated awareness
Big picture/Integrat... ive, out-of-the-box
Inner-directed/Jo...
Transforming the ... elf-talk
People-oriented/C...
Being in the now/Inner ... Long ... rm planning
Power to attract desired ou... mes from within
Transformational or Quiet leadership

Immature

B:
Self-defeat... ctions/Unable to bring things to fruition
Authoritarian/Sense o... ntitlement/Acts of conditional love
Assuming logic to be the key to all knowing/Lost in the details
Rigid, inflexible/Narrow reduc... onist "bottom-line" thinking
Achievement at all cos...
Bulldozing over othe... e communication
... the clock
Trying to fit too muc...
Controlling/Overly compete... ower over" others
Autocratic/Command & control

A:
Lack of self-awareness/Low self-esteem/Directionless
Relationships at all costs/Giving power away/Servile
Superstition/wishful thinking/High level, superficial view
All over the place/Broad, unintegrated thinking
Fun at all costs/Esc...
Mulling over/Sel...
Needing to be li... ver/Unassertive
Unstructured/Pro... planning
Disowns own power/M... ive/Political maneuvering
Unassertive or Manipulative/Playing favorites

I-M

I-F

This is where collectivistic cultures thrive in the dawn of civilization. It is the matriarchal era, where the earlier version of I-F takes a front seat and societies are organized accordingly. It is "pre-personal" because it represents an era prior to the unfoldment of individualism.

In time, the pendulum begins to swing toward I-M. Societies move into the bottom right (B), into what Ken Wilber calls the *Personal Era*. This is where individualistic cultures thrive in the noontime of civilization. It is the patriarchal era, where the earlier version of I-M takes the front seat and societies are organized accordingly. We are well-acquainted with this era.

Then the really interesting part comes.

Societies and individuals begin to tire of the negative consequences of imbalance, especially the negative effects of unbalanced I-M. A strong desire emerges for the reintegration of I-F, only this time, it is mature I-F (C1), which has been maturing all along. However, mature I-F does not represent a singular phase that lasts thousands of years. Awakening mature I-F can almost immediately awaken mature I-M (C2) because these two tend to operate as a dynamic, interconnected duo. Mature I-M is about giving outward expression – through actions and created structures – to the wisdom of mature I-F.

The mature half of the model (C1 and C2) is what Ken Wilber refers to as the *Transpersonal Era*, where dualities are transcended and integrated. This is what we are evolving into right now.

This is an era of higher consciousness, green technology, sustainable living, a respect for human rights, humane and loving relationships with pets and animals, abundance thinking and an emphasis utilizing personal excellence to benefit the greater good.

It marks a significant shift away from dense, ego-based thinking toward greater subtlety and operating from higher levels of consciousness.

APPENDIX C

More Examples of the Zig-Zag Tenet

An ocean liner turns slowly whereas a little speed boat turns on a dime. As an individual your journey to balance is somewhat different from that of society, which is a slow, collective progression over thousands of years.

One major difference is you are in the powerful position to influence your own journey and to see positive results in a relatively short time.

How to progress toward a mature quality

The journey from an immature quality to its mature equivalent *is not a vertical line upward*. It is a curved line upward that represents the integration of the opposite energy *first* before one is able to progress "up."

Here are four detailed examples.

Example 1: Suppose you tend to give your power away in relationships (the immature I-F in relationships). You may be a people-pleaser who tends to put others' needs before your own and/or you may feel that you are not appreciated.

You might yearn for the mature I-F approach to relationships (Figure 3): to have an empathic, caring relationship from a strong sense of self, where your own boundaries are honored.

Figure 3: Moving from immature to mature I-F (relationships)

Mature

I-F
- Self-awareness/Self-esteem/Self-love/Sense of purpose
- **Empathic, caring relationships from a strong sense of self**
- Intuition/Body/Holistic, integrated awareness
- Big picture/Integrating the parts/Creative, out-of-the-box
- Inner-directed/Joy as a state of being
- Transforming the inner environment/Self-talk
- People-oriented/Coaching/Inspiring
- Being in the now/Inner-directed/Long-term planning
- Power to attract desired outcomes from within
- Transformational or Quiet leadership

I-M
- Healthy, self-supporting actions/Able to bring things to fruition
- Partner as equal/Supportive, empowering, loving behavior
- Focused/Differentiating the parts/Methodical, structured
- Detailed knowledge of the parts
- Outer-directed/The joy of achievement
- Transforming the outer environment/Effective communication
- Task-oriented/Mentoring/Delegating (in an empowering way)
- Effective time management/Short term planning
- Power to take action toward desired outcomes/Inclusive power
- Transactional leadership

Intention

- Lack of self-awareness/Low self-esteem/Directionless
- **Relationships at all costs/Giving power away/Servile**
- Superstition/wishful thinking/High level, superficial view
- All over the place/Broad, unintegrated thinking
- Fun at all costs/Escapism/Addictions
- Mulling over/Self-doubt/Depression
- Needing to be liked/Subtly manipulative/Unassertive
- Unstructured/Procrastination/Lack of planning
- Disowns own power/Manipulative/Political maneuvering
- Unassertive or Manipulative/Playing favorites

- Self-defeating actions/Unable to bring things to fruition
- Authoritarian/Sense of entitlement/Acts of conditional love
- Assuming logic to be the key to all knowing/Lost in the details
- Rigid, inflexible/Narrow reductionist "bottom-line" thinking
- Achievement at all costs/Workaholic
- Bulldozing over others/Bullying/Aggressive communication
- Autocratic/Micromanaging/Do it my way
- Trying to fit too much in/Life dictated by the clock
- Controlling/Overly competitive/"Power over" others
- Autocratic/Command & control

Immature

– 206 –

The first step is recognizing that your current state represents an immature I-F way of relating to others.

The way to cultivate mature I-F is to bring in more I-M.

This means embracing more of the individualistic, assertive, "me first" energy that I-M represents – even if you might veer into immature I-M territory for a while. You need to awaken your I-M and it may be necessary to test the boundaries of I-M in order to do so.

There is a Japanese expression that goes something like this: If a reed is leaning too far to the left you must push it too far to the right in order for it to stand up straight.

Your I-M qualities could be embraced by simply deciding to do it and practicing different ways until it becomes a habit. Reading a book or attending a course specifically designed to awaken these qualities could jump-start the process.

To recap, you already have the I-F: the ability to nurture and be caring in relationships. What's missing is your own boundaries and the ability to put your needs first (I-M). Once you integrate more of your I-M you're there. You can then provide an empathic, caring relationship with a strong sense of self and healthy boundaries.

Example 2: Suppose you tend to be dominant or controlling in relationships but you desire a healthy relationship with your intimate partner. There are various possible scenarios this could entail.

You might associate a sense of wellbeing and safety with being in charge or in control. One way of showing it is by buying expensive toys while neglecting the needs of the family.

To maintain an image of strength you might tend to struggle with the vulnerability that comes with showing your feelings, being emotionally honest and experiencing true intimacy with your partner. Controlling yourself in this way provides an illusion of strength which leaves you with few options for showing love other than through actions and structural benefits such as providing.

The first step is recognizing that this represents an immature I-M approach to relationships. The way to cultivate the mature I-M is to bring in more I-F.

Figure 4: Moving from immature to mature I-M (relationships)

Mature

I-M

Healthy, self-supporting actions/Able to bring things to fruition
Partner as equal/Supportive, empowering, loving behavior
Empathic, caring relationships from a strong sense of self
Intuition/Body/Holistic, integrated awareness/Detailed knowledge of the parts
Big picture/Integrating the parts/Creativity/Out-of-the-box/Differentiating the parts/Methodical, structured
Inner-directed/Joy as a state of being/Inner-directed/The joy of achievement
Transforming the inner environment/Self-talk/Transforming the outer environment/Effective communication
People-oriented/Coaching/Inspiring/Task-oriented/Mentoring/Delegating (in an empowering way)
Being in the now/Inner-directed/Long-term planning/Proactive time management/Short term planning
Power to attract desired outcomes from within/Power to take action toward desired outcomes/Inclusive power
Transformational or Quiet leadership/Transactional leadership

Intention ←

Self-defeating actions/Unable to bring things to fruition
Authoritarian/Sense of entitlement/Acts of conditional love
Assuming logic to be the key to all knowing/Lost in the details
Rigid, inflexible/Narrow reductionist "bottom-line" thinking
Achievement at all costs/Workaholic
Bulldozing over others/Bullying/Aggressive communication
Autocratic/Micromanaging/Do it my way
Trying to fit too much in/Life dictated by the clock
Controlling/Overly competitive/ "Power over" others
Autocratic/Command & control

I-F

Self-awareness/Self-esteem/Self-love/Sense of purpose

Lack of self-awareness/Low self-esteem/Directionless
Relationships at all costs/Giving power away/Servile
Superstition/wishful thinking/High level, superficial view
All over the place/Broad, unintegrated thinking
Fun at all costs/Escapism/Addictions
Mulling over/Self-doubt/Depression
Needing to be liked/Subtly manipulative/Unassertive
Unstructured/Procrastination/Lack of planning
Disowns own power/Manipulative/Political maneuvering
Unassertive or Manipulative/Playing favorites

Immature

– 208 –

Coming from immature I-M the necessary shift requires becoming more self-aware, connecting to your heart, learning to cultivate empathy and becoming supportive of your partner's goals and dreams without fear of loss or need for reward. Rather than wanting to control people and outcomes it requires letting go, learning to yield and trusting in your partner and in the wisdom of life itself.

Mature I-M in relationships is about providing a framework of support and taking actions that come from the generosity and tenderness of the heart. This can only happen if the heart is already awakened and the tenderness of the heart can be openly expressed (mature I-F).

Mature I-M is also about treating your partner as an equal even if you "could" be dominant or enjoy certain "privileges" that come with an imagined hierarchy.

What is positive is that you already have the ability to cultivate a sense of personal power by taking action, cultivating a sense of independence and perhaps earning income. You already have awareness of your personal boundaries (e.g. a need for space) and you know how to value your own needs. These are all good in their proper context.

What is needed now is cultivating awareness, opening the heart-space connection, letting go of control, letting go of the need to create hierarchy within the relationship and letting go of unfair "privileges" that are sure to compromise your relationship. These shifts would channel your personal power into the ability to be vulnerable, open and loving as well as providing supportive action in a relationship with an equal.

<u>Example 3</u>: Suppose you tend to handle conflict by retreating from it, mulling over the situation and getting stuck in a depressed state for days or weeks at a time.

Figure 5: Moving from immature to mature I-F (conflict resolution)

Mature

I-F (Mature):
Self-awareness/Self-esteem/Self-love/Sense of purpose
Empathic, caring relationships from a strong sense of self
Intuition/Body/Holistic, integrated awareness
Big picture/Integrating the parts/Creative, out-of-the-box
Inner-directed/Joy as a state of being
Transforming the inner environment/Self-talk
People-oriented/Coaching/Inspiring
Being in the now/Inner-directed/Long-term planning
Power to attract desired outcomes from
Transformational or Quiet leadership

I-M (Mature):
Healthy, self-supporting actions/Able to bring things to fruition
Partner as equal/Supportive, empowering, loving behavior
Logic/Detailed knowledge of the parts
Focused/Differentiating the parts/Methodical, structured
Outer-directed/The joy of achievement
Transforming the outer environment/Effective communication
Task-oriented/Mentoring/Delegating (in an empowering way)
Effective time management/Short term planning
Power to take action toward desired outcomes/Inclusive power
Transitional leadership

Immature

I-F (Immature):
Lack of self-awareness/Low self-esteem/Emotionless
Relationships at all costs/Giving power away/Servile
Superstition/wishful thinking/High level, superficial view
All over the place/Broad, unintegrated thinking
Fun at all costs/Escapism/Addictions
Mulling over/Self-doubt/Depression
Needing to be liked/Subtly manipulative/Unassertive
Unstructured/Procrastination/Lack of planning
Disowns own power/Manipulative/Political maneuvering
Unassertive or Manipulative/Playing favorites

I-M (Immature):
Self-defeating actions/Unable to bring things to fruition
Authoritarian/Sense of entitlement/Acts of conditional love
Applying logic to be the key to all knowing/Lost in the details
Rigid, inflexible/Narrow reductionist "bottom-line" thinking
Achievement at all costs/Workaholic
Bulldozing over others/Bullying/Aggressive communication
Autocratic/Micromanaging/Do it my way
Trying to fit too much in/Life dictated by the clock
Controlling/Overly competitive/"Power over" others
Autocratic/Command & control

Intention

– 210 –

The first step is recognizing that this is the immature I-F way of handling conflict. Rather than being expressed, anger is turned inward, contributing to depression.

The I-F ability to feel emotions is there and this is a good starting point. The way to cultivate mature I-F – the ability to transform the inner environment – is to bring in more I-M.

To get there you need more of an "outward" orientation to your feelings: they need to be expressed.

A good way to do this is to start by journaling about how you feel. This is a way of expressing yourself even if it's only on paper at first. It is a way of getting in touch with and venting your anger (I-M) safely. The purpose is not only a sense of release, but also to become clear about where you stand and where your boundaries lie (I-M). Increasing your levels of physical exercise is another good strategy for releasing your feelings safely.

It is also important to move away from self-blame and crippling self-doubt. This requires bringing in more of the "me first" energy into the equation.

Once you feel clear, it requires self-discipline (I-M) and positive self-talk to stay true to that clarity and refrain from allowing self-doubt to creep in again.

A second element other than self-expression and release requires tapping into your ability to resolve conflicted situations by yourself, within yourself (I-M). I-F is highly relational, and may tend to want to "talk about it" in order to feel better (which in the heat of the moment can make things worse – especially if the other party is not receptive). By contrast I-M is the ability to retreat and resolve things independently.

By the time you talk to the person concerned you are already largely or even fully healed within yourself. You are owning your power because your healing does not depend on the other party. This is one of the most powerful aspects of I-F.

It is not the same as suppressing emotions and keeping an illusion of strength or indifference (that is immature I-M). This is true healing in which emotions are welcomed and addressed. One moves *through* the issue by going through the emotions, not side-stepping them. Only I-F knows how to do this.

To recap, your ability to feel your emotions is there and this is a good starting point. Your ability to be emotionally honest and vulnerable – to see your potential contribution to the situation – is a strength. What is needed now is the self-expression and release along with the clarity of mind and self-discipline (I-M) needed to heal yourself and thus transform your inner environment. This is the precursor to communicating your needs or insights to your partner from a position of inner strength, clarity and healing.

<u>Example 4</u>: Suppose you are hardworking to the point of being a workaholic. You yearn for more in life but seem to be stuck in work mode. The first step is recognizing that workaholism is immature I-M.

Figure 6: Moving from immature to mature I-M (happiness)

Mature

I-F (Mature quadrant):
- Self-awareness/Self-esteem/Self-love/Sense of purpose
- Empathic, caring relationships from a strong sense of self
- Intuition/Body/Holistic, integrated awareness
- Big picture/Integrating the parts/Creative, out-of-the-box
- Inner-directed/Joy as a state of being
- Transforming the inner environment/Self-talk
- People-oriented/Coaching/Inspiring
- Being in the now/Inner-directed/Long-term planning
- Power to attract desired outcomes from within
- Transformational or Quiet leadership

I-M (Mature quadrant):
- Healthy, self-supporting actions/Able to bring things to fruition
- Partner as equal/Supportive, empowering, loving behavior
- Logic/Detailed knowledge of the parts
- Focused/Differentiating the parts/Methodical, structured
- **Outer-directed/The joy of achievement**
- Transforming the outer environment/Effective communication
- Task-oriented/Mentoring/Delegating (in an empowering way)
- Effective time management/Short term planning
- Power to take action toward desired outcomes/Inclusive power
- Transactional leadership

Intention ←

Immature

I-F (Immature quadrant):
- Lack of self-awareness/Low self-esteem/Directionless
- Relationships at all costs/Giving power away/Servile
- Superstition/wishful thinking/High level, subjective view
- All over the place/Broad, unintegrated thinking
- Fun at all costs/Escapism/Addictions
- Mulling over/Self-doubt/Depression
- Needing to be liked/Subtly manipulative/Unassertive
- Unstructured/Procrastination/Lack of planning
- Disowns own power/Manipulative/Political maneuvering
- Unassertive or Manipulative/Playing favorites

I-M (Immature quadrant):
- Self-defeating actions/Unable to bring things to fruition
- Authoritarian/Sense of entitlement/Acts of conditional love
- Assuming logic to be the key to all knowing/Lost in the details
- Rigid, inflexible/Narrow reductionist "bottom-line" thinking
- **Achievement at all costs/Workaholic**
- Bulldozing over others/Bullying/Aggressive communication
- Autocratic/Micromanaging/Do it my way
- Trying to fit too much in/Life dictated by the clock
- Controlling/Overly competitive/"Power over" others
- Autocratic/Command & control

– 213 –

The way to cultivate mature I-M is to bring in more I-F.

One way to do this is by recognizing that workaholism may be a form of escapism. The question is: of what? This requires a courageous process of turning the spotlight inward (I-F) and beginning a process of self-inquiry to become aware of what the emptiness or fear is. A powerful book or course could help kick start the process. This awareness can shift the situation because it places the power back in your hands and enables different choices to be made.

Another way is recognizing that workaholism is an attempt to feel good through constant achievement. This places the source of happiness outside oneself.

I-F offers us happiness as a state of being. It can be cultivated through enhanced self-awareness, surrendering to "what is" and developing an appreciation for every moment. Mindfulness training and learning to be present in the moment very helpful in this journey. Taking a yoga class or learning to meditate are also options as both have a proven track record of increasing endorphins and creating a sense of wellbeing.

Taking up a hobby that purely represents fun (I-F) – not more achievement or competition – is another option. There are many options available. One simply has to be creative.

Once we begin to reconnect with ourselves our own innate wisdom has a chance to come forth (I-F). After that it becomes much harder to take refuge in work as a way to escape our feelings.

With immature I-M we already know the satisfaction of achieving through hard work. That is a positive thing. Moving to a mature I-M approach to work and happiness requires reconnecting to ourselves and cultivating happiness in other ways (I-F). This paves the way for a mature I-M relationship to happiness: to enjoy the achievements that come through work without depending on them for our happiness (or sense of self-worth).

BIBLIOGRAPHY

1. **Byrne, Rhonda.** *The Secret.* New York : Simon and Schuster, 2006.
2. **Hicks, Esther and Jerry.** *Ask and It Is Given: Learning to Manifest Your Desires.* Carlsbad, California : Hay House, Inc, 2004.
3. **Nan Akasha, (Interviewed by Minal Dulashia).** *Living the Awakened Life of True Feminine Power (Online Summit).* April 29, 2014.
4. **Chopra, Deepak.** *Power, Freedom and Grace: Living from the Source of Lasting Happiness.* San Rafael, CA : Amber-Allen Publishing, 2006.
5. **Williamson, Marianne.** *Healing the Soul of America: Reclaiming our Voices as Spiritual Citizens.* s.l. : Simon and Schuster, 2000.
6. **Montana, Cate.** *Unearthing Venus: My search for the woman within.* London : Watkins Publishing, 2013.
7. **Ware, Bronnie.** *The top five regrets of the dying: a life transformed by the dearly departing.* Carlsbad : Hay House, Inc, 2012.
8. **Lippa, Richard A.** *Gender, Nature and Nurture.* New York : Psychology Press, 2005.
9. **John H Zenger, and Joseph R Folkman.** *The extraordinary leader: turning good managers into great leaders.* s.l. : The McGraw-Hill Companies, 2009.
10. **John Mackey, and Raj Sisodia.** *Conscious Capitalism: liberating the heroic spirit of business.* Boston : Harvard Business School Publishing Corporation, 2013.

11. **Ring, Kenneth.** *Lessons from the light.* Portsmouth, NH : Moment Point Press, Inc, 1998.
12. **Rogers, Sandra.** *Lessons From the Light: In-Sights From a Journey to the Other Side.* Atlanta : R. Bemis Publishing, 1995.
13. **Wang, Robin.** Yinyang (Yin-yang). [Online] http://www.iep.utm.edu/yinyang/.
14. **Wikipedia.** Awen. [Online] Jan 21, 2016. [Cited: April 25, 2016.] https://en.wikipedia.org/wiki/Awen.
15. **White, David Gordon.** *Tantra in Practice.* s.l. : Princeton University Press, 2000.
16. **Katherine Anne Harper, Robert L. Brown (eds).** *The Roots of Tantra.* s.l. : State University of New York Press, 2002.
17. **Osho.** *Vigyan Bhairav Tantra Vol 1 - Talks given from 01/10/72 pm to 01/03/73 pm.* 1973.
18. **Elk, Standing.** *Maka Wicahpi Wicohan: Universal and spiritual laws of creation.* Marty, South Dakota : s.n., 1996.
19. **Byskov, Else.** *Death is an illusion: a logical explanation based on Marinus' worldview.* St Paul, MN : Paragon House, 2002.
20. **Samuels, Andrew.** *Jung and the Post-Jungians.* London : Routledge & Kegan Paul plc, 1985.
21. **Montserrat, Dominic.** *Akhenaten: History, fantasy and ancient Egypt.* s.l. : Psychology Press, 2002.
22. **Intersex Society of North America.** Top ten myths. [Online] 2008. [Cited: Mar 2, 2016.] http://www.isna.org/.
23. *Bodily Differences and Collective Identities: The Politics of Gender and Race in Biomedical Research in the United States.* **Epstein, Steven.** 2-3, 2004, Body & Society, Vol. 10, pp. 183-203.
24. **Harrison, Giles.** *Me, Myself and I.* BBC, 2011.
25. **Wheeling, Kate.** The brains of men and women aren't really that different, study finds. *Science.* Nov 30, 2015.
26. **Hicks, Esther.** Hay House Summit 13 June 2014. 2014.
27. **Ross, Alec.** *The industries of the future.* London : Simon and Schuster, 2016.
28. **Katz, Jackson.** Violence against women - its a men's issue. [Online] TED Talks, Nov 2012. [Cited: Mar 23, 2016.] https://

www.ted.com/talks/jackson_katz_violence_against_women_it_s_a_men_s_issue#t-100068.

29. **The World Bank.** *Labor Force, female (% of total labor force).* Washington, DC : World Bank Group, 2015.
30. **US Department of Labor.** Women in the Labor Force (2014). [Online] [Cited: Dec 23, 2015.] http://www.dol.gov/wb/stats/stats_data.htm.
31. **Hochschild, Arlie.** *The Second Shift: working families and the revolution at home.* London : Penguin Books, 2012.
32. **US Department of Labor.** Economic New Release. *Bureau of Labor Statistics.* [Online] 2014. [Cited: 01 04, 2016.] http://www.bls.gov/news.release/atus.t01.htm.
33. **American Association of University Women.** http://www.aauw.org/resource/the-simple-truth-about-the-gender-pay-gap/. [Online] Fall 2015. [Cited: January 4, 2016.] www.aauw.org.
34. **Kollewe, Julia.** http://www.theguardian.com/world/2015/nov/09/gender-pay-gap-women-working-free-until-end-of-year. [Online] The Guardian, November 9, 2015. [Cited: January 4, 2016.] www.theguardian.com.
35. **Heidi Hartmann, Jeffrey Hayes and Jennifer Clark.** *How Equal Pay for Working Women would Reduce Poverty and Grow the American Economy.* Washington DC : Institute for Women's Policy Research, 2014.
36. **Payscale Human Capital.** Do men really earn more than women? [Online] 2012. [Cited: Feb 22, 2016.] http://www.payscale.com/gender-lifetime-earnings-gap#methodology.
37. **Morrison, Ann M and White, Randall P and Van Velsor, Ellen.** *Glass ceiling: can women reach the top of America's largest corporations?* s.l. : Perseus Publishing, 1992.
38. **Chemaly, Soraya.** Why aren't we talking about how boys and men feel about a woman president? [Online] Feb 16, 2016. [Cited: Mar 3, 2016.] http://www.rolereboot.org/culture-and-politics/details/2016-02-arent-talking-boys-men-feel-woman-president/#.VtBlWUvmNWg.twitter.

39. **Egan, Matt.** http://money.cnn.com/2015/03/24/investing/female-ceo-pipeline-leadership/. [Online] March 24, 2015. [Cited: Jan 7, 2016.] http://money.cnn.com.
40. **Yong, Ed.** XY Bias: How Male Biology Students See Their Female Peers. [Online] Feb 16, 2016. [Cited: Feb 26, 2016.] http://www.theatlantic.com/science/archive/2016/02/male-biology-students-underestimate-their-female-peers/462924/.
41. **Sandberg, Cheryl.** *Lean In: Women, Work and the Will to Lead.* New York : Random House, Inc, 2013.
42. **Zaichkowsky, Judith.** Women in the boardroom: one can make a difference. *BNN - Business News Network.* [Online] July 3, 2014. [Cited: January 4, 2016.] http://www.bnn.ca/Video/player.aspx?vid=392193#.U7YJuCrChkU.twitter%20.
43. **Mckinsey & Company.** *Gender diversity: a corporate performance driver.* 2007.
44. **Nagel, Alexandra.** http://www.businesswomen.co.za/one-female-board-member-can-boost-positive-impact/. [Online] 2015.
45. **Heskett, James.** Why Does Lack Of Gender Diversity Hurt A Company's Performance? [Online] Nov 4, 2015. [Cited: Feb 26, 2016.] http://www.forbes.com/sites/hbsworkingknowledge/2015/11/04/why-does-lack-of-gender-diversity-hurt-a-companys-performance/#71c694c34752.
46. **United Nations.** UN Secretary General's Campaign to End Violence Against Women. *http://www.un.org/.* [Online] [Cited: Dec 21, 2015.] http://www.un.org/en/women/endviolence/situation.shtml.
47. **Black, M. C., Basile, K. C., Breiding, M. J., Smith, S. G., Walters, M. L., Merrick, M.** National Intimate Partner and Sexual Violence Survey 2010. *Center for Disease Control and Prevention.* [Online] 2011. http://www.cdc.gov/ViolencePrevention/pdf/NISVS_Report2010-a.pdf.
48. **C.A Rennison, (US Dept of Justice).** Rape and Sexual Assault: Reporting to Police and Medical Attention, 1992 - 2000. *http://www.bjs.gov/.* [Online] 2002. http://www.bjs.gov/content/pub/pdf/rsarp00.pdf.

49. **Association of American Universities.** AAU Campus Survey on Sexual Assault and Sexual Misconduct. *http://www.aau.edu/.* [Online] 2015. http://www.aau.edu/Climate-Survey.aspx?id=16525.

50. **UN Office of the High Commissioner of Human Rights.** [Online] August 2010. http://www.unhcr.org/refworld/docid/4ca99bc22.html.

51. **United Nations.** Fast Facts: Statistics on Violence Against Women and Girls. *UN Women.* [Online] 2014. [Cited: Feb 26, 2016.] http://www.endvawnow.org/en/articles/299-fast-facts-statistics-on-violence-against-women-and-girls-.html.

52. **UN Women.** Facts and Figures: Ending Violence Against Women. *http://www.unwomen.org/.* [Online] 2014. [Cited: Mar 15, 2016.] http://www.unwomen.org/en/what-we-do/ending-violence-against-women/facts-and-figures.

53. **International Center for Research on Women.** Child Marriage Facts and Figures. *http://www.icrw.org/.* [Online] [Cited: Mar 22, 2016.] http://www.icrw.org/child-marriage-facts-and-figures.

54. **United Nations Secretary General's Campaign to End Violence Against Women.** UN Women - Facts and Figures on Violence Against Women. *http://www.un.org.* [Online] 2011. http://www.un.org/en/women/endviolence/situation.shtml.

55. **World Health Organization.** Fact Sheet 241 on Female Genital Mutilation. [Online] Feb 2014. [Cited: Jan 7, 2016.] http://www.who.int/mediacentre/factsheets/fs241/en/.

56. **UN Women.** Secretary General's in-depth Study on all forms of violence against women. *http://www.un.org/womenwatch.* [Online] 2006. [Cited: Jan 7, 2016.] http://www.un.org/womenwatch/daw/vaw/v-sg-study.htm.

57. **Littlejohn, Reggie.** Why gendercide is the real "war" on women. *edition.cnn.com.* [Online] Nov 14, 2014. [Cited: Jan 7, 2016.] http://edition.cnn.com/2014/11/14/opinion/littlejohn-gendercide-women/.

58. **Woodon, Quentin.** Reducing the Gender Gap in Education. [Online] Oct 29, 2014. http://

blogs.worldbank.org/developmenttalk/reducing-gender-gap-education.

59. **Gupta, Pallavi.** Unequal access to education. *Fifth Estate: Achieving Impact.* [Online] July 31, 2014. [Cited: Jan 7, 2016.] http://fifthestateonline.org/unequal-access-to-education/.

60. **UNICEF.** Basic Education and Gender Equality. [Online] 2015. [Cited: Jan 7, 2016.] http://www.unicef.org/education/bege_70640.html.

61. **Institute for Women's Policy Research.** Poverty. [Online] 2016. [Cited: Jan 8, 2016.] http://www.iwpr.org/initiatives/poverty.

62. **United Nations Entity for Gender Equality the Empowerment of Women.** The Feminization of Poverty. [Online] the UN Department of Public Information, May 2000. [Cited: Jan 7, 2016.] http://www.un.org/womenwatch/daw/followup/session/presskit/fs1.htm.

63. **WHO/UNICEF.** *Joint Monitoring Programme for Water Supply and Sanitation, Drinking Water: Equity, Safety and Sustainability, - See more at: http:/Joint Monitoring Programme for Water Supply and Sanitation, Drinking Water: Equity, Safety and Sustainability.* s.l. : WHO/UNICEF, 2012.

64. **UN Women.** Speech by John Hendra on "Feminization of poverty in rural areas". [Online] March 13, 2014. [Cited: Jan 7, 2016.] http:/www.unwomen.org/en/news/stories/2014/3/john-hendra-speech-on-feminization-of-poverty#edn7.

65. **National Coalition of Anti-Violence Programs.** *Lesbian, Gay, Bisexual, Transgender, Queer and HIV-Affected Hate Violence in 2014.* New York : s.n., 2015.

66. **Huffington Post.** 5 things women are judged more harshly for than men. [Online] July 3, 2014. [Cited: Jan 11, 2016.] http://www.huffingtonpost.com/2014/03/07/things-women-judged-for-double-standard_n_4911878.html q.

67. **Zhana Vrangalova, PhD.** Is our sexual double standard going away? [Online] Mar 3, 2014. [Cited: Jan 11, 2016.] https://www.psychologytoday.com/blog/strictly-casual/201403/is-our-sexual-double-standard-going-away.

68. **United Nations.** Statement by the United Nations Working Group on discrimination against women in law and practice. [Online] Oct 18, 2012. [Cited: Jan 11, 2016.] http://www.ohchr.org/EN/NewsEvents/Pages/DisplayNews.aspx?NewsID=12672&LangID=E.
69. **Amnesty International.** Iran: Death by stoning, a grotesque and unacceptable penalty. [Online] Jan 15, 2008. [Cited: Jan 11, 2016.] https://web.archive.org/web/20131020184028/http://www.amnesty.org/en/for-media/press-releases/iran-death-stoning-grotesque-and-unacceptable-penalty-20080115.
70. **Stacy L Smith, Marc Choueiti, Katherine Pieper, Traci Gillig, Carmen Lee and Dylan DeLuca.** *Inequality in 700 popular films: examining portrayals of gender, race & LGBT status from 2007 to 2014.* Los Angeles : University of Southern California, 2015.
71. **Robinson, Ken.** Do schools kill creativity? [Online] Feb 2006. [Cited: Jan 8, 2016.] https://www.ted.com/talks/ken_robinson_says_schools_kill_creativity?language=en.
72. **Hicks, Esther and Jerry.** *The Vortex: Where the Law of Attraction Assembles All Cooperative Relationships.* Carlsbad, CA : Hay House, 2009.
73. **Newell-Hanson, Alice.** Is America having a male identity crisis? [Online] March 16, 2016. [Cited: March 22, 2016.] http://i-d.vice.com/en_us/article/is-america-having-a-male-identity-crisis.
74. **CNN International.** CNN News. February, 2016.
75. **Killerman, Sam.** https://www.youtube.com/watch?v=NRcPXtqdKjE. [Online] May 3, 2013. [Cited: Jan 7, 2016.] https://www.youtube.com/watch?v=NRcPXtqdKjE.
76. **Sweet, Elizabeth.** Toys are more divided by gender now than they were 50 years ago. [Online] Dec 9, 2014. [Cited: Feb 29, 2016.] http://www.theatlantic.com/business/archive/2014/12/toys-are-more-divided-by-gender-now-than-they-were-50-years-ago/383556/.
77. **Ontario consultants on religious tolerance.** Women as clergy. [Online] Dec 30, 2015. [Cited: Feb 29, 2016.] http://www.religioustolerance.org/femclrg13.htm.

78. **Engel, Pamela.** The commander of the anti-ISIS war just denounced Ted Cruz's strategy for fighting the group. [Online] Feb 1, 2016. [Cited: Feb 29, 2016.] http://www.businessinsider.com/ted-cruz-carpet-bomb-strategy-isis-war-macfarland-2016-2.

79. **Engel, Pamela.** Donald Trump: 'I would bomb the s--- out of' ISIS. *Business Insider.* [Online] Nov 13, 2015. [Cited: Feb 29, 2016.] http://www.businessinsider.com/donald-trump-bomb-isis-2015-11.

80. **Ford, Dana.** Who commits mass shootings? [Online] July 24, 2015. [Cited: Feb 29, 2016.] http://edition.cnn.com/2015/06/27/us/mass-shootings/.

81. **Chemaly, Soraya.** Mass killings in the US: masculinity, masculinity, masculinity. [Online] Oct 5, 2015. [Cited: Feb 29, 2016.] http://www.huffingtonpost.com/soraya-chemaly/mass-killings-in-the-us-w_b_8234322.html.

82. **Wikipedia.** Maslow's hierarchy of needs. [Online] April 13, 2016. [Cited: April 26, 2016.] https://en.wikipedia.org/wiki/Maslow%27s_hierarchy_of_needs.

83. **Newsom, Jennifer Siebel.** http://therepresentationproject.org/. [Online] 2015. http://therepresentationproject.org/film/the-mask-you-live-in/about-the-film/.

84. **World Economic Forum.** The Global Gender Gap Report 2015. [Online] 2015. [Cited: April 26, 2016.] http://reports.weforum.org/global-gender-gap-report-2015/rankings/.

85. **Pellissier, Hank.** Feminism's social side effects. [Online] Jan 8, 2011. [Cited: Jan 12, 2011.] http://ieet.org/index.php/IEET/more/pellissier20110108.

86. **Garr, Lisa.** The Aware Show. Los Angeles : Hay House Radio, Sept 26, 2013.

87. **Michael Newton, PH.D.** *Destiny of Souls: New Case Studies of Life Between Lives.* St Paul, MN : Llewellyn Publications, 2000.

88. **Peacock, Louisa.** Women feel need to "act like men" to get ahead at work. [Online] The Telegraph, Sept 13, 2013. [Cited: Jan 14, 2016.] http://www.telegraph.co.uk/women/womens-business/10306864/Women-feel-need-to-act-like-men-to-get-ahead-at-work.html.

89. **Dr Mercola.** Children's health expert panel: Cell phones and Wi-Fi – are children, fetuses and fertility at risk? *www.mercola.com.* [Online] September 21, 2013. [Cited: April 15, 2016.] http://articles.mercola.com/sites/articles/archive/2013/09/21/cell-phone-wifi-radiation.aspx.
90. **Wilber, Ken.** *A brief history of everything.* Boston : Shambala Publications, 2000.

Made in the USA
Las Vegas, NV
11 March 2023

68892535R00142